OF THE IMITATION OF CHRIST

Thomas Hämerken, called Thomas à Kempis from his birthplace, was born at Kempen, near Düsseldorf in Germany, about 1379, was educated at Deventer, and later entered the Augustinian convent at Mount St. Agnes, near Zwolle, in the Netherlands, where he died in 1471. He had a great reputation for sanctity and learning, and wrote much on religious subjects, but it has often been disputed whether he was the author of the one famous book which is traditionally ascribed to him, " Of the Imitation of Christ." At least eighty editions of this appeared between 1470 and 1500, and there have been thousands of editions since, in very many languages.

The first English translation, by Dr. Atkinson, was printed by Pynson in 1503.

OF THE IMITATION OF CHRIST

BY

THOMAS À KEMPIS

Thomas Nelson and Sons Ltd.
London Edinburgh New York
Toronto and Paris

THOMAS NELSON AND SONS LTD
Parkside Works Edinburgh 9
3 Henrietta Street London WC2
312 Flinders Street Melbourne C1
5 Parker's Buildings Burg Street Cape Town

THOMAS NELSON AND SONS (CANADA) LTD
91-93 Wellington Street West Toronto 1

THOMAS NELSON AND SONS
19 East 47th Street New York 17

SOCIÉTÉ FRANÇAISE D'EDITIONS NELSON
25 rue Henri Barbusse Paris V⁰

CONTENTS.

————◆◆————

THE FIRST BOOK.

ADMONITIONS, USEFUL FOR A SPIRITUAL LIFE.

I.	Of the imitation of Christ, and contempt of all the vanities of the world	9
II.	Of thinking humbly of ourselves	11
III.	Of the doctrine of truth	13
IV.	Of wisdom and forethought in our actions	16
V.	Of reading the Holy Scriptures	17
VI.	Of inordinate affections	18
VII.	Of avoiding vain hope and pride	19
VIII.	That too much familiarity is to be shunned	20
IX.	Of obedience and subjection	21
X.	Of avoiding many words	22
XI.	Of the obtaining of peace, and of zealous desire for growth in grace	23
XII.	Of the profit of adversity	26
XIII.	Of resisting temptation	27
XIV.	Of avoiding rash judgment	30
XV.	Of works done out of charity	31
XVI.	Of bearing with the faults of others	33
XVII.	Of life in a religious community	34
XVIII.	Of the examples of the holy fathers	35
XIX.	Of the exercises of a good religious person	38
XX.	Of the love of solitude and silence	42
XXI.	Of compunction of heart	46
XXII.	Of the consideration of human misery	48
XXIII.	Of meditation on death	52
XXIV.	Of judgment, and the punishment of sinners	56
XXV.	Of the zealous amendment of our whole life	61

CONTENTS.

THE SECOND BOOK.

ADMONITIONS CONCERNING INWARD THINGS.

I.	Of the inward life	69
II.	Of humble submission	73
III.	Of a good and peaceable man	74
IV.	Of a pure mind, and a simple intention	76
V.	Of the consideration of one's self	78
VI.	Of the joy of a good conscience	79
VII.	Of the love of Jesus above all things	82
VIII.	Of familiar friendship with Jesus	83
IX.	Of the want of all comfort	86
X.	Of gratitude for the grace of God	90
XI.	That the lovers of the cross of Jesus are few	93
XII.	Of the royal way of the holy cross	95

THE THIRD BOOK.

OF INTERNAL CONSOLATION.

I.	Of Christ's speaking inwardly to the faithful soul	105
II.	That the truth speaketh inwardly without noise of words	106
III.	That the words of God are to be heard with humility, and that many weigh them not	108
IV.	That we ought to live in truth and humility before God	111
V.	Of the wonderful effect of divine love	114
VI.	Of the proving of a true lover	117
VII.	That grace is to be guarded by humility	120
VIII.	Of a mean conceit of ourselves in the sight of God	123
IX.	That all things are to be referred unto God, as their last end	125
X.	That to despise the world and serve God is sweet	126
XI.	That the longings and desires of our hearts are to be examined and moderated	129
XII.	Of the growth of patience in the soul, and of striving against concupiscence	130
XIII.	Of humble obedience after the example of Jesus Christ	133

CONTENTS.

XIV. Of considering the secret judgments of God, that so we be not lifted up for anything good in us . 134

XV. In everything which we desire, how we ought to feel, and what we ought to say. 136

XVI. That true comfort is to be sought in God alone . 138

XVII. That all our anxieties are to be rested on God . 140

XVIII. That temporal sufferings must be borne patiently, after the example of Christ 141

XIX. Of the endurance of injuries, and of the proof of true patience 143

XX. Of the acknowledging of our own infirmities, and of the sufferings of this life. 145

XXI. That we are to rest in God above all his gifts and benefits 148

XXII. Of the remembrance of God's manifold benefits . 151

XXIII. Of four things that bring great inward peace . 154

XXIV. Of avoiding curious inquiry into the lives of others 157

XXV. Wherein firm peace of heart and true spiritual progress consisteth 158

XXVI. Of the excellency of a free mind, which is sooner gained by humble prayer than by study . . 160

XXVII. That it is love of self which most hindereth from the chiefest good 162

XXVIII. Against the tongues of slanderers 164

XXIX. How that we ought to call upon God, and to bless him, when tribulation is upon us 165

XXX. Of craving the divine aid, and of confidence of recovering grace 166

XXXI. Of the contempt of all creatures, in order to find out the Creator 169

XXXII. Of self-denial, and renouncing every evil appetite 172

XXXIII. Of inconstancy of heart, and of having our final intent directed unto God 174

XXXIV. That God is precious above all things, and in all things, to him that loveth him 175

XXXV. That there is no security from temptation in this life 177

XXXVI. Against the vain judgments of men 179

XXXVII. Of pure and entire resignation for the obtaining freedom of heart 181

CONTENTS.

XXXVIII. Of good government of ourselves in things outward, and of recourse to God in dangers . 182

XXXIX. That a man should not be over-careful in matters of business 184

XL. That man hath of himself no good thing, nor anything whereof he can glory 185

XLI. Of the contempt of all temporal honour . 187

XLII. That our peace is not to be set on men . . . 188

XLIII. Against vain and secular knowledge 190

XLIV. Of not attracting to ourselves outward things . 192

XLV. That credit is not to be given to all; and that man is prone to offend in words 193

XLVI. Of putting our trust in God when evil words arise 196

XLVII. That all grievous things are to be endured for the sake of eternal life 198

XLVIII. Of the day of eternity, and this life's straitnesses 200

XLIX. Of the desire of everlasting life, and how great rewards are promised to those that strive resolutely 204

L. How the desolate ought to give up himself into the hands of God 208

LI. That a man ought to employ himself in works of humility, when strength is wanting for higher employment 212

LII. That a man ought not to account himself as worthy of comfort, but rather as deserving of chastisement. 213

LIII. That the grace of God is not given to those who relish earthly things 215

LIV. Of the different stirrings of nature and grace . 217

LV. Of the corruption of nature, and the efficacy of divine grace 221

LVI. That we ought to deny ourselves and imitate Christ by the cross 224

LVII. That a man should not be too much dejected, even when he falleth into some defects . . 227

LVIII. That high matters and God's secret judgments are not to be narrowly inquired into . . 229

LIX. That all our hope and trust are to be fixed in God alone 234

CONTENTS.

THE FOURTH BOOK.

CONCERNING THE COMMUNION.

A devout exhortation to the holy communion 239

I. With how great reverence Christ ought to be received 239

II. That the great goodness and love of God is exhibited to man in this sacrament 245

III. That it is profitable to communicate often . . . 249

IV. That many benefits are bestowed upon those that communicate devoutly 251

V. Of the dignity of this sacrament, and of the ministerial function 255

VI. An inquiry concerning spiritual exercise before communion 257

VII. Of thoroughly searching our own conscience, and of holy purposes of amendment 257

VIII. Of the oblation of Christ on the cross, and of resignation of ourselves 260

IX. That we ought to offer up ourselves and all that is ours unto God, and to pray for all 261

X. That the holy communion is not lightly to be forborne 264

XI. That the body and blood of Christ and the Holy Scriptures are most necessary unto a faithful soul 268

XII. That he who is about to communicate with Christ ought to prepare himself with great diligence . 272

XIII. That the devout soul ought with the whole heart to seek union with Christ in this sacrament . . 274

XIV. Of the fervent desire of some devout persons to receive the body and blood of Christ 277

XV. That the grace of devotion is obtained by humility and denial of ourselves 278

XVI. That we ought to lay open our necessities to Christ, and to crave his grace 280

XVII. Of fervent love, and vehement desire to receive Christ 282

XVIII. That a man should not be a curious searcher into the holy sacrament, but an humble follower of Christ, submitting his sense to divine faith 284

THE FIRST BOOK.
ADMONITIONS, USEFUL FOR A SPIRITUAL LIFE.

OF THE
IMITATION OF CHRIST.

———◆———

THE FIRST BOOK.

ADMONITIONS, USEFUL FOR A SPIRITUAL LIFE.

———

CHAPTER I.

*Of the Imitation of Christ, and Contempt of all
the Vanities of the World.*

HE that followeth me walketh not in darkness,[1]
saith the Lord. These are the words of Christ,
by which we are taught to imitate his life and
manners, if we would be truly enlightened, and be
delivered from all blindness of heart. Let therefore our chief endeavour be to meditate upon the
life of JESUS Christ.

2. The doctrine of Christ exceedeth all the doctrines of holy men ; and he that hath the Spirit will
find therein the hidden manna.

But it falleth out that many, albeit they often
hear the gospel of Christ, are yet but little affected,
because they have not the Spirit of Christ.

[1] John viii. [12].

Whosoever then would fully and feelingly understand the words of Christ, must endeavour to conform his life wholly to the life of Christ.

3. What will it avail thee to be engaged in profound reasonings concerning the Trinity, if thou be
void of humility, and art thereby displeasing to the
Trinity ?

Surely great words do not make a man holy and
just ; but a virtuous life maketh him dear to God.

I had rather FEEL compunction than know the
definition thereof.

If thou knewest the whole Bible by heart, and the
sayings of all the philosophers, what would it profit
thee without the love of God [1] and without grace ?

Vanity of vanities, all is vanity,[2] except to love
God, and him only to serve.

This is the highest wisdom, by contempt of the
world to tend towards the kingdom of Heaven.

4. It is therefore vanity to seek after perishing
riches, and to trust in them.

It is also vanity to strive after honours, and to
climb to high degree.

It is vanity to follow the desires of the flesh, and
to labour for that for which thou must afterwards
suffer grievous punishment.

It is vanity to desire to live long, and not to care
to live well.

It is vanity to mind only this present life, and not to
make provision for those things which are to come.

It is vanity to love that which speedily passeth
away, and not to hasten thither where everlasting
joy awaiteth thee.

[1] 1 Cor. xiii. [2].   [2] Eccles. i. [2].

5. Call often to mind that proverb, " The eye is not satisfied with seeing, nor the ear filled with hearing." [1]

Endeavour therefore to withdraw thy heart from the love of visible things, and to turn thyself to the invisible.

For they that follow their lusts stain their own consciences, and lose the grace of God.

CHAPTER II.

Of Thinking Humbly of Ourselves.

ALL men naturally desire knowledge ; [2] but what availeth knowledge without the fear of God ?

Surely an humble husbandman that serveth God is better than a proud philosopher who, neglecting himself, is occupied in studying the course of the heavens.

Whoso knoweth himself is lowly in his own eyes, and delighteth not in the praises of men.

If I understood all things in the world, and had not charity, what would it avail me in the sight of God, who will judge me according to my deeds ?

2. Cease from an inordinate desire of knowledge, for therein is much distraction and deceit.

Learned men are anxious to seem learned to others, and to be called wise.[3]

There be many things to know which doth little or nothing profit the soul : and he is very unwise

[1] Eccles. i. [8].   [2] Eccles. i. [13] ; Arist. Met. I. 1.   [3] 1 Cor. iii. [1].

who minds other things more than those that tend to his salvation.

Many words do not satisfy the soul; but a good life comforteth the mind, and a pure conscience giveth great confidence toward God.

3. The more thou knowest, and the better thou understandest, the more strictly shalt thou be judged, unless thy life be also the more holy.

Be not therefore elated in thine own mind because of any art or science, but rather let the knowledge given thee make thee afraid.

If thou thinkest that thou understandest and knowest much; yet know that there be many more things which thou knowest not.

Affect not to be overwise, but rather acknowledge thine own ignorance.[1]

Why wilt thou prefer thyself before others, seeing there be many more learned, and more skilful in the Scripture than thou?

If thou wilt know or learn anything profitably, desire to be unknown, and to be little esteemed.

4. The highest and most profitable lesson is the true knowledge and lowly esteem of ourselves.

It is great wisdom and perfection to think nothing of ourselves, and to think always well and highly of others.

If thou shouldest see another openly sin, or commit some heinous offence, yet oughtest thou not to think the better of thyself; for thou knowest not how long thou shalt be able to stand.

We are all frail,[2] but do thou esteem none more frail than thyself.

[1] Rom. xii. [16].   [2] Gen. viii. [21].

CHAPTER III.

Of the Doctrine of Truth.

HAPPY is he whom truth by itself doth teach,[1] not by figures and words that pass away, but as it is in itself.

Our own opinion and our own sense do often deceive us, and they discern but little.

What availeth it to cavil and dispute much about dark and hidden things,[2] for ignorance of which we shall not be reproved at the day of judgment?

It is a great folly to neglect the things that are profitable and necessary, and to choose to dwell upon that which is curious and hurtful. We have eyes and see not.[3]

2. And what have we to do with *genera* and *species?* He to whom the Eternal Word speaketh is delivered from many an opinion.

From one Word are all things, and all things utter one word; and this is the *Beginning*, which also speaketh unto us.

No man without that Word understandeth or judgeth rightly.

He to whom all things are one, he who reduceth all things to one, and seeth all things in one, may enjoy a quiet mind, and remain at peace in God.

O God, who art the truth, make me one with thee in everlasting love.

It wearieth me often to read and hear many things: in thee is all that I would have and can desire.

---

[1] Ps. xciv. [12].   [2] Eccles. iii. [9–11].   [3] Ps. cxv. [5].

Let all doctors hold their peace ; let all creatures be silent in thy sight ; speak thou alone unto me.

3. The more a man is at one within himself, and becometh of single heart, so much the more and higher things doth he understand without labour ; for that he receiveth the light of wisdom from above.[1]

A pure, single, and stable spirit is not distracted, though it be employed in many works ; for that it doeth all to the honour of God, and being at rest within, seeketh not itself in anything it doth.

Who hinder and trouble thee more than the un-mortified affections of thine own heart ?

A good and devout man arrangeth within himself beforehand those things which he ought to do.

Neither do they draw him to the desires of an inordinate inclination, but he ordereth them according to the direction of right reason.

Who hath a greater combat than he that laboureth to overcome himself ?

This ought to be our endeavour, to conquer ourselves, and daily to wax stronger, and to grow in holiness.

4. All perfection in this life hath some imperfection mixed with it ; and no knowledge of ours is without some darkness.

A humble knowledge of thyself is a surer way to God than a deep search after learning.

Yet learning is not to be blamed, nor the mere knowledge of anything whatsoever, for that is good in itself, and ordained by God ; but a good conscience and a virtuous life are always to be preferred before it.

[1] Matt. xi. [25] ; Luke x. [21].

But because many endeavour rather to get knowledge than to live well, therefore they are often deceived, and reap either none or but little fruit.

5. Oh, if men bestowed as much labour in the rooting out of vices, and the planting of virtues, as they do in the moving of questions, neither would so many evils be done, nor so great scandal be given in the world.

Truly, at the day of judgment we shall not be examined as to what we have read, but as to what we have done ; [1] not as to how well we have spoken, but as to how religiously we have lived.

Tell me, where are all those doctors and masters, with whom thou wast well acquainted, whilst they lived and flourished in learning ?

Others occupy their places, and perhaps do scarce ever think of those who went before them. In their lifetime they seemed something, but now they are not spoken of.

6. Oh, how quickly doth the glory of the world pass away ! [2] Would that their life had been answerable to their learning ! then had their study and reading been to good purpose.

How many perish by reason of vain learning [3] of this world, who take little care of the serving of God.

And because they rather choose to be great than humble, therefore they become vain in their imaginations.[4]

He is truly great who hath great love.

He is truly great that is little in himself, and that maketh no account of any height of honour.[5]

[1] Matt. xxv.   [2] Eccles. ii. [11].   [3] Titus i. [10].
[4] Rom. i. [21].   [5] Matt. xviii. [4] ; xxiii. [11].

He is truly wise that accounteth all earthly things as dung, that he may win Christ.[1]

And he is truly learned that doeth the will of God, and forsaketh his own will.

CHAPTER IV.

Of Wisdom and Forethought in our Actions.

WE must not trust every saying or suggestion,[2] but warily and patiently ponder things according to the will of God.

Yet, alas! such is our weakness, that we often rather believe and speak evil of others than good.

But perfect men do not easily credit every one who speaks to them; for they know that human frailty is prone to evil,[3] and very subject to error in words.[4]

2. It is great wisdom not to be rash in thy doings,[5] nor to stand stiffly in thine own conceits;

As also not to believe everything which thou hearest, nor immediately to relate again to others[6] what thou hast heard or dost believe.

Consult with him that is wise and of sound judgment, and seek to be instructed by one better than thyself, rather than to follow thine own inventions.[7]

---

[1] Phil. iii. [8].   [2] 1 John iv. [1].   [3] Gen. viii. [21].
[4] James iii. [2].   [5] Prov. xix. [2].   [6] Prov. xvii. [9].
                          [7] Prov. xii. [15].

A good life maketh a man wise according to God,[1] and giveth him experience in many things.[2]

The more humble a man is in himself, and the more subject unto God, the more wise and peaceful shall he be in all things.

CHAPTER V.

Of Reading the Holy Scriptures.

TRUTH, not eloquence, is to be sought for in Holy Scripture.

Each part of the Scripture is to be read with the same Spirit wherewith it was written.[3]

We should rather search after profit in the Scriptures, than after subtle arguments.

We ought to read plain and devout books as willingly as those high and profound.

Let not the authority of the writer be a stumbling-block, whether he be of great or small learning; but let the love of pure truth draw thee to read.[4] Inquire not who spoke this or that, but mark what is spoken.

2. Men pass away, but the truth of the Lord remaineth for ever.[5] God speaks unto us in sundry ways without respect of persons.[6] Our own curiosity often hindereth us in reading of the Scriptures, when we will examine and discuss that which we should rather pass over without more ado.

[1] Prov. xv. [33]. [2] Eccles. i. [16]. [3] Rom. xv. [4].
[4] 1 Cor. ii. [4]. [5] Ps. cxvii. [2]; Luke xxi. [33].
[6] Rom. ii. [11], x. [12]; Col. iii. [11].

If thou desire to profit, read with humility, simplicity, and faithfulness ; nor ever desire the repute of learning.

Inquire willingly, and hear with silence the words of holy men.   Let not the parables of the elders displease thee, for they are not given without cause.[1]

CHAPTER VI.

Of Inordinate Affections.

WHENSOEVER a man desireth anything inordinately, he becometh presently disquieted in himself.

The proud and covetous can never rest. The poor and humble in spirit dwell in the multitude of peace.

The man that is not yet perfectly dead to himself, is quickly tempted and overcome in small and trifling things.

The weak in spirit, and he that is yet in a manner carnal and prone to the things of sense, can hardly withdraw himself altogether from earthly desires.

And therefore he is often afflicted when he goeth about to withdraw himself from them, and is easily angered when any opposeth him.

2. And if he hath followed his appetite, he is presently disquieted with remorse of conscience ; for that he hath yielded to his passion, which profiteth him nothing to the obtaining of the peace which he sought.

[1] Prov. i. [6] ; Eccles. xii. [9].

True quietness of heart therefore is gotten by resisting our passions, not by obeying them.

There is then no peace in the heart of a carnal man, nor in him that is given to outward things, but in the spiritual and devout man.

CHAPTER VII.

Of Avoiding Vain Hope and Pride.

HE is vain that putteth his trust in man,[1] or in creatures.

Be not ashamed to serve others for the love of JESUS Christ, nor to be esteemed poor in this world.

Presume not upon thyself, but place thy hope in God.[2]

Do what lieth in thy power, and God will assist thy good will.

Trust not in thine own knowledge,[3] nor in the skill of any living creature ; but rather in the grace of God, who helpeth the humble, and humbleth those that are proud.

2. Glory not in wealth if thou have it, nor in friends because they are powerful ; but in God who giveth all things, and who desireth to give thee himself above all things.

Esteem not thyself for the height of thy stature nor for the beauty of thy person, which may be disfigured and destroyed by a little sickness.

Please not thyself in thy natural gifts or wit,

[1] Jer. xvii. [5].   [2] Ps. xxxi. [1].   [3] Jer. ix. [23].

lest thereby thou displease God, to whom appertaineth all the good whatsoever thou hast by nature.

3. Esteem not thyself better than others,[1] lest
perhaps in the sight of God, who knoweth what
is in man, thou be accounted worse than they.

Be not proud of well-doing ;[2] for the judgment
of God is far different from the judgment of men,
and that often offendeth him which pleaseth them.

If there be any good in thee, believe that there
is much more in others, that so thou mayest preserve
humility.

It hurteth thee not to submit to all men ; but it
hurteth thee most of all to prefer thyself even to
one.

The humble enjoy continual peace, but in the
heart of the proud is envy, and frequent indignation.

CHAPTER VIII.

That too much Familiarity is to be Shunned.

LAY not thy heart open to every one ; but treat
of thy affairs with the wise, and such as fear God.[3]

Converse not much with the young, nor with
strangers.[4]

Flatter not the rich ; neither do thou appear
willingly before the great.

Keep company with the humble and single-
hearted, with the devout and virtuous ; and confer

[1] Ex. iii. [11].   [2] Job ix. [20].
[3] Eccles. viii. [12].   [4] Prov. v. [10].

with them of those things that may edify. Be not familiar with any woman ; but commend all good women in general to God.

Desire to be familiar alone with God and his angels, and avoid the acquaintance of men.

2. We must have love towards all, but familiarity with all is not expedient.

Sometimes it falleth out that a person unknown to us is much esteemed of, from the good report given him by others, whose presence notwithstanding is not grateful to the eyes of those who see him.

We think sometimes to please others by our society, and we rather displease them with those bad qualities which they discover in us.

CHAPTER IX.

Of Obedience and Subjection.

It is a great matter to live in obedience, to be under a superior and not to be at our own disposing.

It is much safer to obey than to govern.

Many live under obedience, rather for necessity than for love ; such are discontented, and do easily repine. Neither can they attain to freedom of mind, unless they willingly and heartily put themselves under obedience for the love of God.

Go whither thou wilt, thou shalt find no rest, but in humble subjection under the government of a superior. Many have deceived themselves, imagining to find happiness in change.

2. True it is that every one willingly doeth that which agreeth with his own liking, and inclineth most to those that are of his own mind.

But if God be amongst us, we must sometimes cease for the sake of peace to adhere to our own opinion.

Who is so wise that he can fully know all things ?

Be not therefore too confident in thine own opinion, but be willing to hear the judgment of others.

If thy thought be good, and yet thou partest with it for God, and followest the opinion of another, this shall turn to thy good.

3. I have often heard that it is safer to hear and to take counsel than to give it.

It may also fall out that a man's opinion may be good ; but to refuse to yield to others when reason or a special cause requireth it, is a mark of pride and stiffness.

CHAPTER X.

Of Avoiding Many Words.

FLY the tumult of the world as much as thou canst ;[1] for the treating of worldly affairs is a great hindrance, although it be done with sincere intention.

For we are quickly defiled, and enthralled by vanity.

Oftentimes I could wish that I had held my peace when I have spoken ; and that I had not been in company.

[1] Matt. iv. [1], xiv. [23] ; John vi. [15].

Why do we so willingly speak and talk one with another, when notwithstanding we seldom cease our converse before we have hurt our conscience ? [1]

The cause why we so willingly talk, is for that by discoursing one with another, we seek to receive comfort one of another, and desire to ease our mind wearied with many thoughts :

And we very willingly talk and think of those things which we most love or desire, or of those things which we feel to be against us.

2. But, alas, oftentimes in vain, and to no end ; for this outward comfort is the cause of no small loss of inward and divine consolation.

Therefore we must watch and pray, lest our time pass away idly.

If it be lawful and expedient for thee to speak, speak those things that may edify.

Evil habit and neglect of our own growth in grace do give too much liberty to inconsiderate speech.

Yet discourse of spiritual things doth greatly further our spiritual growth, especially when persons of one mind and spirit associate together in God. [2]

CHAPTER XI.

Of the Obtaining of Peace, and of Zealous Desire for Growth in Grace.

WE might enjoy much peace, if we would not busy ourselves with the words and deeds of other men,

[1] Matt. vii. [1]; Rom. ii. [1].   [2] Acts i. [14]; Rom. xv. [5, 6].

and with things which appertain nothing to our charge.

How can he abide long in peace who thrusteth himself into the cares of others, who seeketh occasions abroad, who little or seldom cometh to himself?

Blessed are the single-hearted, for they shall enjoy much peace.

2. Why were some of the saints so perfect and contemplative? Because they laboured to mortify themselves wholly to all earthly desires; and therefore they could with their whole heart fix themselves upon God, and be free for holy retirement.

We are too much led by our passions, and too solicitous for transitory things.

We also seldom overcome any one vice perfectly, and are not inflamed with a fervent desire to grow better every day; and therefore we remain cold and lukewarm.

3. If we were perfectly intent upon our own hearts, and not entangled with outward things, then should we be able to relish divine things, and to have some experience of heavenly contemplation.

The greatest, and indeed the whole impediment is that we are not free from passions and lusts, neither do we endeavour to walk in the perfect way of the saints; and when but a small adversity befalleth us, we are too quickly dejected, and turn ourselves to human consolations.

4. If we would endeavour like brave men to stand in the battle, surely we should feel the assistance of God from heaven.

For he who giveth us occasion to fight, to the

CHAPTER XIII.

Of Resisting Temptation.

So long as we live in this world we cannot be without tribulation and temptation.

Hence it is written in Job, " The life of man upon earth is a life of temptation."

Every one therefore ought to be careful about his temptations, and to watch in prayer, lest the devil find an advantage to deceive him ; for he never sleepeth, but goeth about, seeking whom he may devour.

No man is so perfect and holy but he hath sometimes temptations, and we cannot be altogether without them.

2. Nevertheless temptations are often very profitable to us, though they be troublesome and grievous ; for in them a man is humbled, purified, and instructed.

All the saints passed through man's tribulations and temptations, and profited thereby.

And they that could not bear temptations became reprobate, and fell away.

There is no order so holy, nor place so secret, as that there be not temptations or adversities in it.

3. There is no man that is altogether free from temptations whilst he liveth on earth : for the root thereof is in ourselves, who are born with inclination to evil.

When one temptation or tribulation goeth away, another cometh ; and we shall ever have something to suffer, because we are fallen from the state of our felicity.

Many seek to fly temptations, and fall more grievously into them.

By flight alone we cannot overcome, but by patience and true humility we become stronger than all our enemies.

4. He that only avoideth them outwardly, and doth not pluck them up by the roots, shall profit little; yea, temptations will the sooner return unto him, and will be more violent than before.

By little and little, and by patience with long-suffering, through God's help, thou shalt more easily overcome, than by violence and thine own disquietude.

Often take counsel in temptations, and deal not roughly with him that is tempted; but give him comfort, as thou wouldest wish to be done to thyself.

5. The beginning of all evil temptations is inconstancy of mind, and small confidence in God.

For as a ship without a helm is tossed to and fro by the waves, so the man who is careless and forsaketh his purpose is many ways tempted.

Fire trieth iron, and temptation a just man.

We know not oftentimes what we are able to do, but temptation shows us what we are.

Yet we must be watchful, especially in the beginning of the temptation; for the enemy is then more easily overcome, if he be not suffered to enter the door of our hearts, but be resisted at the very gate, on his first knocking.

Wherefore one said, "Withstand the beginnings: the remedy is applied too late, when the evil has grown strong through long delay." [1]

[1] Ovid, Lib. xiii. de Remed. Am.

For first there cometh to the mind a bare thought of evil, then a strong imagination thereof, afterwards delight, and evil motion, and then consent.

And so by little and little our wicked enemy getteth complete entrance, for that he is not resisted in the beginning.

And the longer a man is negligent in resisting, the weaker does he become daily in himself, and the stronger the enemy against him.

6. Some suffer great temptations in the beginning of their conversion ; others in the latter end.

Others again are much troubled almost through the whole of their life.

Some are but slightly tempted, according to the wisdom and equity of the Divine appointment, which weigheth the states and deserts of men, and ordaineth all things for the welfare of his own chosen ones.

7. We ought not therefore to despair when we are tempted, but so much the more fervently to pray unto God, that he will vouchsafe to help us in all tribulations ; for he will surely, according to the words of St. Paul, make with the temptation a way to escape, that we may be able to bear it.[1]

Let us therefore humble our souls under the hand of God in all temptations and tribulations, for he will save and exalt the humble in spirit.

8. In temptations and afflictions a man is proved, how much he hath profited ; and his reward is thereby the greater, and his graces do more eminently shine forth.

Neither is it any such great thing if a man be

[1] 1 Cor. x. [13].

devout and fervent, when he feeleth no affliction ; but if in time of adversity he bear himself patiently, there is hope then of great growth in grace.

Some are kept from great temptations, and in small ones which do daily occur are often overcome ; to the end that, being humbled, they may never presume on themselves in great matters, while they are worsted in so small things.

CHAPTER XIV.

Of Avoiding Rash Judgment.

Turn thine eyes unto thyself, and beware thou judge not the deeds of other men.[1] In judging of others a man laboureth in vain, often erreth, and easily sinneth ; [2] but in judging and examining himself, he always laboureth fruitfully.

We often judge of things according as we fancy them ; for private affection bereaves us easily of a right judgment.

If God were always the pure object of our desire, we should not be so easily troubled, through the repugnance of our carnal mind.

2. But oftentimes something lurketh within, or else occurreth from without, which draweth us after it.

Many secretly seek themselves in what they do, and know it not.

They seem also to live in good peace of mind, when things are done according to their will and opinion ;

---

[1] Matt. vii. [1] ; Rom. xv. [1].   [2] Eccles. iii. [16].

but if things happen otherwise than they desire, they are straightway moved and much vexed.

The diversities of judgments and opinions cause oftentimes dissensions between friends and countrymen, between religious and devout persons.[1]

3. An old custom is hardly broken,[2] and no man is willing to be led farther than himself can see.

If thou dost more rely upon thine own reason or industry than upon that power which brings thee under the obedience of JESUS Christ, it will be long before thou become illuminated ; for God will have us perfectly subject unto him, that, being inflamed with his love, we may transcend the narrow limits of human reason.

CHAPTER XV.

Of Works Done out of Charity.

FOR no worldly thing, nor for the love of any man, is any evil to be done ; [3] but yet, for the welfare of one that standeth in need, a good work is sometimes to be intermitted without any scruple, or even to be changed for a better.

For by doing this, a good work is not lost, but changed into a better.

Without charity the outward work profiteth nothing ; [4] but whatsoever is done of charity, be it never so little and contemptible in the sight of the world, it becomes wholly fruitful.

---

[1] Matt. xii. [25] ; Luke xii. [51].   [2] Jer. xiii. [23].
[3] Matt. xviii. [8].   [4] 1 Cor. xiii. [3] ; Luke vii. [47].

For God weigheth more with how much love a man worketh, than how much he doeth. He doeth much that loveth much.

2. He doeth much that doeth a thing well. He doeth well that rather serveth the common weal than his own will.[1]

Oftentimes a work seemeth to be of charity, and it is rather a work of the flesh ; because natural inclination, self-will, hope of reward, and desire of our own interest are motives seldom absent.

3. He that hath true and perfect charity, seeketh himself in nothing ;[2] but only desireth in all things that the glory of God should be exalted.

He also envieth none, because he seeketh no private good ; neither doth he will to rejoice in himself, but wisheth above all things to be made happy in the enjoyment of God.[3]

He attributeth nothing that is good to any man, but wholly referreth it unto God, from whom as from their fountain all things proceed ; in whom finally all the saints do rest as in their highest fruition.

If a man had but one spark of true charity, he would certainly discern that all earthly things are full of vanity.

[1] Phil. ii. [17].   [2] Phil. ii. [21] ; 1 Cor. xiii. [5].
[3] Ps. xvii. [15], xxiv. [6].

CHAPTER XVI.

Of Bearing with the Faults of Others.

THOSE things that a man cannot amend in himself or in others, he ought to suffer patiently, until God order them otherwise.

Think that perhaps it is better so for thy trial and patience, without which all our good deeds are not much to be esteemed.

Thou oughtest to pray, notwithstanding when thou hast such impediments, that God would vouchsafe to help thee, and that thou mayest bear them rightly.[1]

2. If one that is once or twice warned will not give over, contend not with him ; but commit all to God, that his will may be done,[2] and his name honoured in all his servants, who well knoweth how to turn evil into good.

Endeavour to be patient in bearing with the defects and infirmities of others, of what sort soever they be : for that thyself also hast many failings which must be borne with by others.[3]

If thou canst not make thyself such an one as thou wouldest, how canst thou expect to have another in all things to thy liking ?

We would willingly have others perfect, and yet we amend not our own faults.

3. We will have others severely corrected, and will not be corrected ourselves.

The large liberty of others displeaseth us ; and yet we will not have our own desires denied us.

[1] Matt. vi. [13] ; Luke xi. [4].   [2] Matt. vi. [10].
[3] I Thess. v. [14] ; Gal. vi. [1].

We will have others kept under by strict laws; but in no sort will ourselves be restrained.

And thus it appeareth, how seldom we weigh our neighbour in the same balance with ourselves.

If all men were perfect, what should we have to suffer of our neighbour for the sake of God?

4. But now God hath thus ordered it, that we may learn to bear one another's burdens:[1] for no man is without fault; no man but hath his burden; no man is sufficient of himself; no man is wise enough of himself; but we ought to bear with one another, comfort one another, help, instruct, and admonish one another.[2]

Occasions of adversity best discover how great virtue or strength each one hath.

For occasions do not make a man frail, but they show what he is.

CHAPTER XVII.

Of Life in a Religious Community.

THOU must learn to break thine own will in many things if thou wilt have peace and concord with others.[3]

It is no small matter to dwell in a religious community or monastery, to hold thy place there without giving offence, and to continue faithful even unto death.[4]

---

[1] Gal. vi. [2].   [2] 1 Thess. v. [14]; 1 Cor. xii. [25].
[3] Gal. vi. [1].   [4] Luke xvi. [10].

Blessed is he that hath there lived well, and ended happily.

If thou wilt stand firm and grow as thou oughtest, esteem thyself as a pilgrim and stranger upon earth.[1]

Thou must be contented for Christ's sake to be esteemed as a fool in this world, if thou desire to lead the life of a monk.

2. Dress and tonsure profit little ; but change of heart and perfect mortification of the passions make a true monk.

He that seeketh anything else, but merely God, and the salvation of his soul, shall find nothing but tribulation and sorrows.[2]

Neither can he remain long in peace, that laboureth not to be the least, and subject unto all.

3. Thou camest to serve, not to rule.[3] Know that thou wast called to suffer and to labour, and not to be idle, nor to spend thy time in talk.

Here therefore men are proved as gold in the furnace.

Here no man can stand, unless he humble himself with his whole heart for the love of God.

CHAPTER XVIII.

Of the Examples of the Holy Fathers.

CONSIDER the lively examples of the holy fathers, in whom true perfection and religion shone,[4] and

[1] 1 Peter ii. [11]. [2] Eccles. i. [17, 18] ; Ecclus. i. [18].
[3] Matt. xx. [26]. [4] Heb. xi.

thou shalt see how little it is, and almost nothing, which we do now in these days.

Alas! what is our life, if we be compared to them!

The saints and friends of Christ served the Lord in hunger and thirst, in cold and nakedness, in labour and weariness, in watchings and fastings, in prayer and holy meditations, in many persecutions and reproaches.

2. Oh how many and grievous tribulations suffered the apostles, martyrs, confessors, virgins, and all the rest that endeavoured to follow the steps of Christ! For they hated their lives in this world, that they might keep them unto life eternal.[1]

Oh how strict and self-renouncing a life led those holy fathers in the wilderness![2] How long and grievous temptations suffered they! How often were they assaulted by the enemy! What frequent and fervent prayers offered they to God! What rigorous abstinences did they use! How great zeal and care had they of their spiritual advancement! How strong a combat had they for the overcoming of their lusts! What pure and upright intentions kept they towards God!

In the day they laboured, and in the night they attended to continual prayer; although even while they laboured, they never ceased from mental prayer.

3. They spent all their time with profit; every hour seemed but short for the service of God. And by reason of the great sweetness they felt in contemplation, they forgot the necessity of refreshment for the body.

[1] John xii. [25].   [2] Matt. vii. [14].

They renounced all riches, dignities, honours, friends, and kinsfolk ; [1] they desired to have nothing which appertained to the world ; they scarce took the necessaries of life ; they grudged even the necessary care of the body.

Therefore they were poor in earthly things, but very rich in grace and virtues.

Outwardly they were destitute, but inwardly they were refreshed with grace and divine consolation.

4. They were strangers to the world, but near and familiar friends to God.[2]

They seemed to themselves as nothing, and to this present world despicable ; but were precious and beloved in the eyes of God.

They were grounded in true humility, they lived in simple obedience, they walked in love and patience ; and therefore they grew daily in the Spirit, and obtained great grace in God's sight.

They were given for an example to all religious persons ; [3] and they should more provoke us to endeavour after spiritual advancement, than the number of the lukewarm livers should prevail to make us remiss.

5. Oh how great was the fervour of all religious persons in the beginning of their holy institution !

How great was their devotion to prayer ! What ambition to excel others in virtue ! What exact discipline then flourished ! How great reverence and obedience, under the rule of their superiors, observed they in all things !

Their footsteps yet remaining testify that they

[1] Matt. xix. [29].   [2] James iv. [4].
[3] Used here to signify persons living under a monastic rule.

were indeed holy and perfect men, who fighting so valiantly trod the world under their feet.

Among us he is greatly accounted of who is not a transgressor, and who can with patience endure that which he hath received.

6. Oh the lukewarmness and negligence of our times! that we so quickly decline from the ancient fervour, and are come to that pass, that very sloth and lukewarmness of spirit make our life tedious unto us.

Would to God the desire to grow in virtues did not wholly sleep in thee, who hast often seen the many examples of religious persons!

CHAPTER XIX.

Of the Exercises of a Good Religious Person.

THE life of a good religious person ought to excel in all virtues; [1] that he may inwardly be such as outwardly he seemeth to men.

And rightly there ought to be much more within than is perceived without. For God beholdeth us; [2] whom we are bound most highly to reverence wheresoever we are, and to walk in purity [3] like angels in his sight.

Daily ought we to renew our purposes, and to stir up ourselves to greater fervour, as though this were the first day of our conversion; and to say,—

" Help me, my God, in this my good purpose, and

[1] Matt. v. [48].   [2] Ps. xxxiii. [13]; Heb. iv. [12, 13].   [3] Ps. xv. [2].

in thy holy service ; and grant that I may now this day begin perfectly ; for that which I have done hitherto is as nothing."

2. According to our purpose shall be the success of our spiritual profiting ; and much diligence is necessary to him that will profit much.

And if he that firmly purposeth often faileth, what shall he do that seldom or but weakly purposeth anything ?

Yet in various ways it happens that we forsake our purpose, and a slight omission of our spiritual exercises is not without loss to our souls.

The purpose of just men depends not upon their own wisdom, but upon God's grace ; on whom they always rely for whatsoever they take in hand.

For man proposes, but God disposes ; [1] neither is the way of man in himself.

3. If an accustomed exercise be sometimes omitted, either for some act of piety, or profit to our brother, it may easily afterwards be recovered again.

But if, out of weariness or carelessness, we lightly omit it, it is very blameworthy, and will be felt to be hurtful. Do the best we can, we shall still too easily fail in many things. [2]

Yet must we always have some fixed purpose, and especially against those sins which do most of all hinder us.

We must diligently search into and set in order both our outward and inward things, because both of them are of importance to our progress in godliness.

4. If thou canst not continually collect thyself,

[1] Prov. xvi. [9].   [2] Eccles. vii. [20].

yet do it sometimes, at the least twice a day—namely, in the morning and at night.

In the morning fix thy good purpose; and at night examine thyself what thou hast done, how thou hast behaved thyself, in word, deed, and thought;[1] for in these perhaps thou hast oftentimes offended both God and thy neighbour.

Gird up thy loins like a man against the vile assaults of the devil; bridle thy riotous appetite, and thou shalt be the better able to keep under all the unruly motions of the flesh.

Never be entirely idle; but either be reading, or writing, or praying, or meditating, or endeavouring something for the public good.

As for bodily exercises, they must be used with discretion; neither are they to be practised of all men alike.

5. Those devotions which belong not to the community ought not to be exposed to public view; for private devotions are practised most safely in secret.

Nevertheless thou must beware thou neglect not those which are public, being more ready for what is private. But having fully and faithfully accomplished all which thou art bound and enjoined to do, if thou hast any spare time, betake thee to thyself, as thy devotion calleth thee.

All cannot use one kind of spiritual exercise, but one is more useful for this person, another for that.

According to the seasonableness of times also, divers exercises are fitting; some suit better with us on working days, others on holy days.

[1] Deut. iv.

In the time of temptation, we have need of some, and of others in time of peace and quietness.

Some suit us when we are pensive, and others when we rejoice in the Lord.

6. About the time of the chief festivals, good exercises are to be renewed, and the prayers of godly saints more fervently to be implored.

From festival to festival we should purpose, as though we were then to depart out of this world, and to come to the everlasting festival.

Therefore ought we carefully to prepare ourselves at holy times, and to live more devoutly, and to keep more exactly all things that we are to observe, as though we were shortly at God's hands to receive the reward of our labours.

7. But if that reward be deferred, let us think with ourselves that we are not sufficiently prepared, and unworthy yet of so great glory which shall be revealed in us [1] in due time ; and let us endeavour to prepare ourselves better for our departure.

" Blessed is that servant (saith the evangelist St. Luke) whom his Lord when he cometh shall find watching : Verily, I say unto you, he shall make him ruler over all his goods." [2]

[1] Rom. viii. [18].   [2] Luke xii. [43, 44] ; Matt. xxiv. [46, 47].

CHAPTER XX.

Of the Love of Solitude and Silence.

SEEK a convenient time [1] of leisure for thyself, and meditate often upon God's loving-kindness.

Meddle not with things too high for thee, but read such things as may rather yield compunction to thy heart than occupation to thy head.

If thou wilt withdraw thyself from speaking vainly, and from gadding idly, as also from hearkening after novelties and rumours, thou shalt find leisure enough and suitable for meditation on good things.

The greatest saints avoided the society of men,[2] when they could conveniently; and did rather choose to live to God in secret.

2. One said, "As oft as I have been among men, I returned home less a man than I was before." [3]

And this we find true, when we talk long together. It is easier not to speak at all, than not to exceed in speech.

It is easier for a man to lie hid at home, than to be able sufficiently to watch over himself abroad.

He therefore that intends to attain to the more inward and spiritual things of religion, must with JESUS depart from the multitude and press of people.[4]

No man doth safely appear abroad but he who can abide at home.

No man doth safely speak but he that is glad to hold his peace.[5]

---

[1] Eccles. iii. [1].   [2] Heb. xi. [38].   [3] Seneca, Ep. vii.
[4] Matt. v. [1].   [5] Eccles. ii. [7].

No man doth safely rule but he that is glad to be ruled.

No man doth safely rule but he that hath learned gladly to obey.

3. No man rejoiceth safely unless he hath within him the testimony of a good conscience.

And yet always the security of the saints was full of the fear of God.

Neither were they the less anxious and humble in themselves, for that they shone outwardly with grace and great virtues.

But the security of bad men ariseth from pride and presumption, and in the end it deceiveth them.

Although thou seem to be a good religious person, or a devout solitary, yet never promise thyself security in this life.

4. Oftentimes those who have been in the greatest esteem and account amongst men, have fallen into the greatest danger, by overmuch self-confidence.

Wherefore to many it is more profitable not to be altogether free from temptations, but to be often assaulted, lest they should feel too safe, and so perhaps be puffed up with pride ; or else should too freely give themselves to worldly comforts.

Oh how good a conscience would he keep, that would never seek after transitory joy, nor ever entangle himself with the world !

Oh what great peace and quietness would he possess, that would cut off all vain anxiety, and think only upon divine things, and such as are profitable for his soul, and would place all his confidence in God !

5. No man is worthy of heavenly comfort unless

he have diligently exercised himself in holy compunction.

If thou desirest true contrition of heart, enter into
thy secret chamber, and shut out the tumults of the
world, as it is written, " Commune with your own
heart, and in your chamber, and be still." [1] In thy
chamber thou shalt find what abroad thou shalt too
often lose.

The more thou visitest thy chamber, the more
thou wilt enjoy it ; the less thou comest thereunto,
the more thou wilt loathe it. If in the beginning of
thy conversion thou art content to remain in it, and
keep to it well, it will afterwards be to thee a dear
friend, and a most pleasant comfort.

6. In silence and in stillness a religious soul ad-
vantageth itself, and learneth the mysteries of Holy
Scripture.

There it findeth rivers of tears, wherein it may every
night [2] wash and cleanse itself ; that it may be so much
the more familiar with its Creator, by how much the
farther off it liveth from all worldly disquiet.

Whoso therefore withdraweth himself from his
acquaintance and friends, God will draw near unto
him with his holy angels.

It is better for a man to live privately, and to have
regard to himself, than to neglect his soul, though he
could work wonders in the world.

It is commendable in a religious person seldom to
go abroad, to be unwilling to see or to be seen.

7. Why art thou desirous to see that which it
is unlawful for thee to have ? The world passeth
away and the lust thereof.

[1] Ps. iv. [4].　　[2] Ps. vi. [6].

The lusts of the flesh draw us to rove abroad ; but when the time is past, what carriest thou home with thee but a burdened conscience and a distracted heart ?

A merry going forth bringeth often a mournful return ; and a joyful night maketh often a sad morning.[1]

So all carnal joy enters gently, but in the end it bites and stings to death.

What canst thou see elsewhere which thou canst not see here ? [2] Behold the heaven and the earth and all the elements ; for of these are all things created.

8. What canst thou see anywhere that can long continue under the sun ?

Thou thinkest perchance to satisfy thyself, but thou canst never attain it.

Couldst thou see all things present before thine eyes, what were it but a vain sight ? [3]

Lift up thine eyes [4] to God in the highest, and pray him to pardon thy sins and negligences.

Leave vain things to the vain ; but be thou intent upon those things which God hath commanded thee.

Shut thy door upon thee,[5] and call unto thee JESUS, thy Beloved.

Stay with him in thy closet ; for thou shalt not find so great peace anywhere else.

If thou hadst not gone abroad and hearkened to idle rumours, thou wouldst the better have preserved a happy peace of mind. But since thou delightest sometimes to hear new things, it is but fit thou suffer for it some disquietude of heart.

---

[1] Prov. xiv. [13]. [2] Eccles. i. [10]. [3] Eccles. iii. [11].
[4] Ps. cxxi. [1]. [5] Matt. vi. [6].

CHAPTER XXI.

Of Compunction of Heart.

IF thou wilt make any progress in godliness, keep thyself in the fear of God,[1] and affect not too much liberty. Restrain all thy senses under discipline, and give not thyself over to foolish mirth.

Give thyself to compunction of heart, and thou shalt gain much devotion thereby.

Compunction layeth open much good, which dissoluteness is wont quickly to destroy.

It is a wonder that any man can ever perfectly rejoice in this life if he duly consider, and thoroughly weigh his state of banishment, and the many perils wherewith his soul is environed.

2. Through levity of heart, and small care for our failings, we feel not the real sorrows of our souls; and so oftentimes we vainly laugh, when we have just cause to weep.

There is no true liberty nor right joy but in the fear of God accompanied with a good conscience.

Happy is he who can cast off all distracting impediments, and bring himself to the one single purpose of holy compunction.

Happy is he who can abandon all that may defile his conscience or burden it.

Contend manfully; one habit overcometh another.

If thou canst let others alone in their matters, they likewise will not hinder thee in thine.

[1] Prov. xix. [23].

3. Busy not thyself in matters which appertain to others, neither do thou entangle thyself with the affairs of thy betters.

Still have an eye to thyself first, and be sure more especially to admonish thyself before all thy friends.

If thou hast not the favour of men, be not grieved at it ; [1] but take this to heart, that thou dost not behave thyself so warily and circumspectly as it becometh the servant of God, and a devout religious man.

It is better oftentimes and safer that a man should not have many consolations in this life, [2] especially such as are according to the flesh.

But that we have not divine consolations at all, or do very seldom taste them, the fault is ours, because we seek not after compunction of heart, nor do altogether forsake the vain and outward comforts of this world.

4. Know that thou art unworthy of divine consolation, and that thou hast rather deserved much tribulation.

When a man hath perfect compunction, then is the whole world grievous and bitter unto him. [3]

A good man findeth always sufficient cause for mourning and weeping.

For whether he consider his own or his neighbour's estate, he knoweth that none liveth here without tribulation.

And the more narrowly a man looketh into himself, so much the more he sorroweth.

Our sins and wickednesses wherein we lie so

[1] Gal. i. [10].   [2] Ps. lxxvi. [5].
[3] Judges ii. [4], xx. [26] ; 2 Kings xiii.

enwrapt that we can seldom apply ourselves to heavenly contemplations, do minister unto us matter of just sorrow and inward compunction.

5. Didst thou oftener think of thy death [1] than of length of life, there is no question but thou wouldst be more zealous to amend.

If also thou didst but consider within thyself the infernal pains in the other world,[2] I believe thou wouldst willingly undergo any labour or sorrow in this world, and not be afraid of the greatest austerity.

But because these things enter not the heart, and we still love those things only that delight us, therefore it is we remain cold and very dull in religion.

6. It is often our want of spirituality which maketh our miserable body so easily to complain.

Pray therefore unto the Lord with all humility, that he will vouchsafe to give thee the spirit of compunction. And say with the prophet, " Feed me, O Lord, with the bread of tears, and give me plenteousness of tears to drink." [3]

CHAPTER XXII.

Of the Consideration of Human Misery.

MISERABLE thou art, wheresoever thou be, or whithersoever thou turnest, unless thou turn thyself unto God.

[1] Eccles. vii. [1, 2]. [2] Matt. xxv. [41]. [3] Ps. lxxx. [5].

Why art thou troubled when things succeed not as thou wouldst or desirest ? For who is he that hath all things according to his mind ? [1] neither I nor thou, nor any man upon earth.

There is none in this world, even though he be king or bishop, without some tribulation or perplexity.

Who is then in the best case ? even he who is able to suffer something for God.

2. Many weak and infirm persons say, Behold ! what a happy life such an one leads ; [2] how wealthy, how great he is, in what power and dignity !

But lift up thine eyes to the riches of heaven, and thou shalt see that all the goods of this life are nothing to be accounted of. They are very uncertain, and rather burdensome than otherwise, because they are never possessed without anxiety and fear.

Man's happiness consisteth not in having abundance of temporal goods,[3] but a moderate portion is sufficient for him.

Truly it is misery even to live upon the earth.[4]

The more spiritual a man desires to be, the more bitter does this present life become to him ; because he sees more clearly and perceives more sensibly the defects of human corruption.

For to eat and to drink, to sleep and to watch, to labour and to rest, and to be subject to other necessities of nature, is doubtless a great misery and affliction to a religious man, who would gladly be set loose, and freed from all sin.

3. For the inward man is much weighed down in this world by the needs of the body.

---

[1] Eccles. vi. [2].   [2] Luke xii. [19].
[3] Prov. xix. [1].   [4] Job xiv. [1]; Eccles. ii. [17].

Therefore the prophet prayeth with great devotion to be enabled to be free from them, saying, " Bring thou me out of my distresses." [1]

But woe be to them that know not their own misery ; and a greater woe to them that love this miserable and corruptible life ! [2]

For some there be who so much dote upon it, that although by labour or by begging they can scarce get mere necessaries, yet if they might be able to live here always, they would care nothing at all for the kingdom of God.

4. Oh how senseless are these men and unbelieving in heart, who lie so deeply sunk in the earth that they can relish nothing but carnal things ! [3]

But miserable as they are, they shall in the end feel to their cost how vile and how nothing that was which they loved.

Whereas the saints of God and all the devour friends of Christ regarded not those things which pleased the flesh, nor those which were in repute in this life, but longed after the everlasting riches [4] with their whole hope and earnest effort.

Their whole desire was carried upward to things durable and invisible, that the desire of things visible might not draw them to things below.

5. O my brother, cast not away thy confidence of making progress in godliness ; there is yet time, the hour is not yet past. [5]

Why wilt thou defer thy good purpose from day to day ？ Arise and begin in this very instant, and

---

[1] Ps. xxv. [17].   [2] Rom. viii. [22].
[3] Rom. viii. [5].   [4] 1 Peter i. [4] ; Heb. xi. [26].
[5] Rom. xiii. [11] ; Heb. x. [35].

say, Now is the time to be doing, now is the time to be striving, now is the fit time to amend myself.

When thou art ill at ease and much troubled, then is the time of earning thy reward.

Thou must pass through fire and water [1] before thou come to a wealthy place.

Unless thou doest violence to thyself, thou shalt never get the victory over sin.

So long as we carry about us this frail body of ours, we can never be without sin, nor live without weariness and pain.

We would gladly have rest from all misery, but seeing that by sin we have lost our innocency, we have together with that lost also the true felicity. [2]

Therefore it becomes us to have patience, and to wait for the mercy of God, till this tyranny be overpast, and mortality be swallowed up of life. [3]

6. Oh how great is human frailty, which is always prone to evil! [4]

To-day thou confessest thy sins, and to-morrow thou committest the very same which thou hast confessed.

Now, thou art purposed to look well into thy ways, and within a while thou so behavest thyself as though thou hadst never any such purpose at all.

Good cause have we therefore to humble ourselves, [5] and never to have any great conceit of ourselves, since we are so frail and so inconstant.

That also may quickly be lost by our own negligence, which, by the grace of God, with much labour we have scarce at length obtained.

---

[1] Ps. xlvi. [12].   [2] Rom. vii. [24]; Gen. iii. [17].
[3] 2 Cor. v. [4].   [4] Gen. vi. [5], viii. [21].   [5] 2 Mac. ix. [11].

7. What will become of us in the end, who begin so early to wax lukewarm ?

Woe be unto us, if we will so give ourselves unto ease as if all were now peace and safety, when as yet there appeareth no sign of true holiness in our conversation !

We have much need like young novices to be newly instructed again to good life, if haply there be some hope of future amendment, and greater proficiency in things spiritual.

CHAPTER XXIII.

Of Meditation on Death.

VERY quickly there will be an end of thee here ; [1] see therefore to thy state : to-day man is ; to-morrow he is gone.

And when he is out of sight, quickly also is he out of mind.

Oh the stupidity and hardness of man's heart, which thinketh only upon the present, and doth not rather care for what is to come !

Thou oughtest so to order thyself in all thy thoughts and actions as if to-day thou wert to die. [2]

If thou hadst a good conscience, thou wouldst not greatly fear death. [3]

It were better to avoid sin than to escape death. [4]

[1] Job ix. [25, 26], xiv. [1, 2]; Luke xii. [20]; Heb. ix. [27].
[2] Matt. xxv. [13].   [3] Luke xii. [37].   [4] Wisd. iv. [16].

If to-day thou art not prepared, how wilt thou be so to-morrow ? [1]

To-morrow is uncertain, and how knowest thou that thou shalt live till to-morrow ?

2. What availeth it to live long, when there is so small amendment in us ?

Alas ! length of days doth not always better us, but often rather increaseth our sin.

Oh that we had spent but one day in this world thoroughly well !

Many there are who reckon years of conversion, and yet full slender oftentimes is the fruit of amendment.

If to die be accounted dreadful, to live long may perhaps prove more dangerous.

Happy is he that always hath the hour of his death before his eyes,[2] and daily prepareth himself to die.

If at any time thou hast seen another man die, make account that thou must also pass the same way.[3]

3. When it is morning, think that thou mayest die before night ;

And when evening comes, dare not to promise thyself the next morning.

Be thou therefore always in readiness, and so lead thy life that death may never take thee unprepared.[4]

Many die suddenly and when they look not for it ; for the Son of man will come in an hour when we think not.[5]

---

[1] Matt. xxiv. [44], xxv. [10].   [2] Eccles. vii. [1].   [3] Heb. ix. [27].
[4] Luke xxi. [36].   [5] Matt. xxiv. [44] ; Luke xii. [40].

When that last hour shall come, thou wilt begin to have a far different opinion of thy whole life that is past, and be exceeding sorry that thou hast been so careless and remiss.

4. Oh how wise and happy is he that now laboureth to be such an one in his life, as he will desire to be found at the hour of death !

A perfect contempt of the world,[1] a fervent desire to go forward in all virtue, a love of discipline, a laborious repentance, a ready obedience, a denying of ourselves, and an endurance of any affliction whatsoever for the love of Christ, will give us great confidence that we shall die happily.

Whilst thou art in health, thou mayest do much good ; but when thou art sick, I see not what thou wilt be able to do.

Few by sickness grow better and more reformed ; so also they who wander much abroad, seldom thereby become holy.

5. Trust not to friends and kindred, neither do thou put off the care of thy soul's welfare till hereafter ; for men will forget thee sooner than thou art aware of.

It is better to look to it betime, and to send some good before thee, than to trust to other men's help.[2]

If thou be not careful for thyself now, who will be careful for thee hereafter ?

Time now is very precious : now is the day of salvation ; now is the accepted time.

But alas that thou shouldst spend time so idly here, in which thou mightest purchase life eternal !

[1] Ecclus. xli. [1].
[2] Isa. xxx. [5], xxxi. [1] ; Jer. xvii. [5], xlviii. [7] ; Matt. vi. [20].

The time will come when thou shalt desire one day or hour to amend in, and I know not that it will be granted thee.

6. O beloved, from how great danger mightest thou deliver thyself, from how great fear free thyself, if thou wouldst be ever fearful and mindful of death!

Labour now so to live that at the hour of death thou mayest rather rejoice than fear.

Learn now to die to the world, that thou mayest then begin to live with Christ.[1]

Learn now to contemn all things,[2] that thou mayest then freely go to Christ.

Chastise thy body now by repentance,[3] that thou mayest then have assured confidence.

7. Ah, fool! why dost thou think to live long, when thou canst not promise to thyself one day?[4]

How many have been deceived and suddenly snatched away!

How often dost thou hear these reports, Such a man is slain, another man is drowned, a third has broken his neck with a fall from some high place, this man died eating, and that man playing! One perished by fire, another by the sword, another of the plague, another was slain by thieves. Thus death is the end of all, and man's life suddenly passeth away like a shadow.[5]

8. Who shall remember thee when thou art dead? and who shall pray for thee?

Do now, even now, my beloved, whatsoever thou art able to do; for thou knowest not when thou

---

[1] Rom. vi. [1].   [2] Luke xiv. [33].   [3] 1 Cor. ix. [27].
[4] Luke xii. [20].   [5] Job xiv. [2].

shalt die, nor yet what shall befall thee after thy death.

Now, whilst thou hast time, heap unto thyself everlasting riches.[1]

Think on nothing but the salvation of thy soul, care for nothing but the things of God.

Make now friends to thyself by honouring the saints of God, and imitating their actions, that when thou failest they may receive thee into everlasting habitations.[2]

9. Keep thyself as a stranger and pilgrim upon the earth,[3] who hath nothing to do with the affairs of this world.

Keep thy heart free, and lifted up to God, because thou hast here no abiding city.[4]

Send thither thy daily prayers and sighs together with thy tears, that after death thy spirit may be found worthy to pass in felicity to the Lord. *Amen.*

CHAPTER XXIV.

Of Judgment, and the Punishment of Sinners.

In all things look to the end, and see how thou wilt be able to stand before that severe Judge[5] from whom nothing is hid, who is not pacified with gifts, nor admitteth any excuses, but will judge according to right.

[1] Matt. vi. [20]; Luke xii. [33]; Gal. vi. [8].
[2] Luke xvi. [9]; Heb. xi. [3] 1 Peter ii. [11].
[4] Heb. xiii. [14].   [5] Heb. x. [31].

O wretched and foolish sinner, who sometimes fearest the countenance of an angry man, what answer wilt thou make to God, who knoweth all thy wickedness ! [1]

Why dost thou not provide for thyself [2] against that great day of judgment, when no man can excuse or answer for another, but every one shall have enough to answer for himself ?

Now may thy pains profit, thy tears be accepted,[3] thy groans be heard, thy grief may bring thee peace, and purge thy soul.

2. The patient man hath a great and wholesome purgatory,[4] who though he receive injuries, yet grieveth more for the malice of another, than for his own suffering ; who prayeth willingly for his adversaries,[5] and from his heart forgiveth their offences. He delayeth not to ask forgiveness of whomsoever he hath offended ; he is sooner moved to compassion than to anger ; he often offereth violence to himself, and laboureth to bring his body wholly into subjection to the spirit.

It is better to purge out our sins, and cut off our vices here, than to keep them to be punished hereafter.

Verily we do but deceive ourselves through an inordinate love of the flesh.

3. What is there that the fire of hell shall feed upon but thy sins ?

The more thou sparest thyself now, and followest the flesh, the more severe hereafter shall be thy punishment, and thou storest up greater fuel for that flame.

---

[1] Job ix. [2].   [2] Luke xvi. [9].   [3] 2 Cor. vi. [4].
[4] James i. [4].   [5] Luke xxiii. [34]; Acts vii. [60].

In what things a man hath sinned, in the same shall he be the more grievously punished.

There shall the slothful be pricked forward with burning goads, and the gluttons be tormented with extreme hunger and thirst.

There shall the luxurious and lovers of pleasure be bathed in burning pitch and stinking brimstone, and the envious, like mad dogs, shall howl for very grief.

4. There is no sin but shall have its own proper torment.

There the proud shall be filled with all confusion; the covetous shall be pinched with miserable penury.

One hour of pain there shall be more bitter than a thousand years of the sharpest penance here!

There is no quiet, no comfort for the damned there;[1] yet here we have some intermission of our labours, and enjoy the comfort of our friends.

Be now solicitous and sorrowful because of thy sins, that at the day of judgment thou mayest be secure with the blessed.

For then shall the righteous with great boldness stand against such as have vexed and oppressed them.[2]

Then shall he stand to judge them who doth now humbly submit himself to the censures of men.

Then shall the poor and humble have great confidence, but the proud man shall be compassed with fear on every side.

5. Then will it appear that he was wise in this

---

[1] Job xl. [12], xli. [2] Wisd. v. [1].

world who had learned to be a fool and despised for Christ's sake.

Then shall every affliction patiently undergone delight us, when the mouth of all iniquity shall be stopped.[1]

Then shall all the devout rejoice, and all the profane mourn.

Then shall the mortified flesh more rejoice than that which hath been pampered with all pleasures.[2]

Then shall the poor attire shine gloriously, and the precious robes seem vile and contemptible.

Then the poor cottage shall be more commended than the gilded palace.

Then shall constant patience more avail us than all earthly power.

Then simple obedience shall be exalted above all worldly wisdom.[3]

6. Then shall a good and clear conscience more rejoice a man than all the learning of philosophy.

Then shall the contempt of riches weigh more than all the worldling's treasure.

Then shalt thou be more comforted that thou hast prayed devoutly than that thou hast fared daintily.

Then shalt thou be more glad that thou hast kept silence than that thou hast spoken much.

Then shall good works avail more than many goodly words.

Then a strict life and severe repentance shall be more pleasing than all earthly delights.

Accustom thyself now to suffer a little, that thou mayest then be delivered from more grievous pains.

[1] Ps. cvii. [42].   [2] 2 Cor. iv. [17].   [3] Isa. xxix. [19].

Prove first here what thou canst endure hereafter.

If now thou canst endure so little, how wilt thou then be able to support eternal torments ?

If now a little suffering make thee so impatient, what will hell fire do hereafter ?

Assure thyself thou canst not have two joys ; it is impossible to take thy pleasure here in this world, and after that to reign with Christ.

7. Suppose that thou hadst up to this day lived always in honours and delights, what would it all avail thee if thou wert doomed to die at this instant ? [1]

All therefore is vanity,[2] except to love God and serve him only.

For he that loveth God with all his heart is neither afraid of death, nor of punishment, nor of judgment, nor of hell ; for perfect love gives secure access to God.[3]

But he that takes delight in sin, what marvel is it if he be afraid both of death and judgment ?

Yet it is good, although love be not yet of force to withhold thee from sin, that at least the fear of hell should restrain thee.

But he that layeth aside the fear of God can never continue long in good estate, but falleth quickly into the snares of the devil.

---

[1] Luke xii. [20].   [2] Eccles. i. [2].   [3] Rom. viii. [39].

CHAPTER XXV.

Of the Zealous Amendment of our Whole Life.

BE watchful and diligent in the service of God;[1] and often bethink thyself wherefore thou camest hither, and why thou hast left the world. Was it not that thou mightest live to God, and become a spiritual man?

Be fervent then in going forward,[2] for shortly thou shalt receive the reward of thy labours; there shall not be then any more fear or sorrow in thy coasts.[3]

Labour but a little now, and thou shalt find great rest, yea, perpetual joy.[4]

If thou continuest faithful and fervent in thy work, no doubt but that God will be faithful and liberal in rewarding thee.[5]

Thou oughtest to have a good hope[6] of getting the victory; but thou must not be secure, lest thou wax either negligent or proud.

2. When one that was in anxiety of mind, often wavering between fear and hope, did once, being oppressed with grief, humbly prostrate himself in a church before the altar, in prayer, and said within himself, Oh, if I knew that I should yet persevere! he presently heard within him an answer from God, which said, If thou didst know it, what wouldst thou do? Do now what thou wouldst do then, and thou shalt be secure.

And being herewith comforted and strengthened,

---

[1] 2 Tim. iv. [5].   [2] Matt. v. [48].   [3] Rev. xxi. [4], xxii. [3].
[4] Ecclus. li. [27]; Rev. xxi. [4], xxii. [3].   [5] Matt. xxv. [23].
[6] Rom. v. [5].

he committed himself wholly to the will of God, and his anxious wavering ceased.

Neither had he the mind to search curiously any further, to know what should befall him ; but rather laboured to understand what was the perfect and acceptable will of God [1] for the beginning and accomplishing of every good work.

3. " Trust in the Lord, and do good," saith the prophet ; " so shalt thou dwell in the land, and verily thou shalt be fed." [2]

One thing there is that draweth many back from a spiritual progress, and the diligent amendment of their lives : the fear of the difficulty, or the labour of the combat.

But they especially exceed others in all virtue who make the greatest effort to overcome those things which are most grievous and contrary unto them.

For there a man improveth most and obtaineth greatest grace, where he most overcometh himself and mortifieth himself in spirit.

4. But all men have not equally much to overcome and mortify.

Yet he that is zealous and diligent, though he have more passions, shall profit more than another that is of a more temperate natural disposition, if he be less fervent in the pursuit of all virtue.

Two things especially much further our amendment—to wit, To withdraw ourselves violently from those vices to which our nature is most inclined, and to labour earnestly for that good which we most lack.

Be careful also to avoid with great diligence those

[1] Rom. xii. [2].   [2] Ps. xxxvii. [3].

things in thyself which do commonly displease thee
in others.

5. Gather some profit to thy soul wheresoever
thou art; so that if thou seest or hearest of any
good examples, thou stir up thyself to the imitation
thereof.

But if thou observe anything worthy of reproof,
beware thou do not the same. And if at any time
thou hast done it, labour quickly to amend thyself.

As thine eye observeth others,[1] so art thou also
noted again by others.

Oh how sweet and pleasant a thing it is to see
brethren fervent and devout, well-mannered and
well-disciplined![2]

And on the contrary, how sad and grievous a
thing it is to see them live in a dissolute and disordered sort, not applying themselves to that for
which they are called!

How hurtful a thing is it, when they neglect the
good purposes of their vocation, and busy themselves in that which is not committed to their care!

6. Be mindful of the profession which thou hast
made, and have always before the eyes of thy soul
the remembrance of thy Saviour crucified.

Thou hast good cause to be ashamed in looking
upon the life of JESUS Christ, seeing thou hast not as
yet endeavoured to conform thyself more unto him,
though thou hast been a long time in the way of
God.

A religious person that exerciseth himself seri-
ously and devoutly in the most holy life and passion
of our Lord, shall there abundantly find whatsoever

[1] Matt. vii. [3].   [2] Eph. v.; 1 Cor. xii. [18]; Eccles. iii. [1].

is necessary and profitable for him ; neither shall he need to seek any better thing *out* of JESUS.

Oh, if JESUS crucified would come into our hearts,[1] how quickly and fully should we be taught !

7. A fervent religious person taketh and beareth well all that is commanded him.

But he that is negligent and lukewarm hath tribulation upon tribulation, and on all sides is afflicted ; for he is void of inward consolation, and is forbidden to seek outward comforts.

A religious person that liveth not according to discipline, lieth open to great mischief, to the ruin of his soul.

He that seeketh liberty and ease shall ever live in disquiet, for one thing or other will displease him.

8. Oh that we had nothing else to do, but always with our mouth and whole heart to praise our Lord God !

Oh that thou mightest never have need to eat, or drink, or sleep ; but mightest always praise God, and only employ thyself in spiritual exercises. Thou shouldest then be much more happy than now thou art, when for so many necessities thou art constrained to serve thy body !

Would God there were not these necessities, but only the spiritual refreshments of the soul, which, alas, we taste too seldom !

9. When a man cometh to that estate, that he seeketh not his comfort from any creature, then doth he begin perfectly to relish God. Then shall he be contented with whatsoever doth befall him.

[1] Gal. ii. [20], vi. [14].

Then shall he neither rejoice in having much, nor be sorrowful for having little ; but entirely and confidently commit himself to God, who shall be unto him all in all ;[1] to whom nothing doth perish nor die, but all things do live unto him, and serve him at his command without delay.

10. Remember always thine end,[2] and that time lost never returns. Without care and diligence thou shalt never get virtue.

If thou begin to wax lukewarm,[3] it will begin tc be evil with thee.

But if thou give thyself to fervour of spirit, thou shalt find much peace, and feel less labour, by reason of the assistance of God's grace, and the love of virtue.

The fervent and diligent man is prepared for all things.

It is harder work to resist vices and passions, than to toil in bodily labours.

He that avoideth not small faults, by little and little falleth into greater.[4]

Thou wilt always rejoice in the evening, if thou have spent the day profitably.

Be watchful over thyself, stir up thyself, admonish thyself, and whatever becomes of others neglect not thyself.

The more violence thou usest against thyself, the greater shall be thy profiting. *Amen.*

[1] Rom. xi. [36] ; 1 Cor. viii. [6], xii. [6], xv. [28].
[2] Ecclus. vii. [36].   [3] Rev. iii. [16].   [4] Ecclus. xix. [1].

THE SECOND BOOK.
ADMONITIONS CONCERNING INWARD THINGS.

THE SECOND BOOK.

CHAPTER I.

Of the Inward Life.

THE kingdom of God is within you,[1] saith the Lord. Turn thee with thy whole heart [2] unto the Lord, and forsake this wretched world, and thy soul shall find rest.

Learn to despise outward things, and to give thyself to things inward, and thou shalt perceive the kingdom of God to be come in thee.

" For the kingdom of God is peace and joy in the Holy Ghost," [3] which is not given to the unholy.

Christ will come unto thee, and show thee his own consolation, if thou prepare for him a worthy mansion within thee.

All his glory and beauty is from within,[4] and there he delighteth himself.

The inward man he often visiteth ; and hath with him sweet discourses, pleasant solace, much peace, familiarity exceeding wonderful.

[1] Luke xvii. [21].   [2] Joel ii. [12].   [3] Rom. xiv. [17].
[4] Ps. xlv. [13].

2. O faithful soul, make ready thy heart for this Bridegroom, that he may vouchsafe to come unto thee, and to dwell within thee.

For thus saith he, " If any man love me, he will keep my words, and we will come unto him, and will make our abode with him." [1]

Give therefore admittance unto Christ, and deny entrance to all others.

When thou hast Christ, thou art rich, and hast enough. He will be thy faithful and provident helper in all things, so that thou shalt not need to trust in men.

For men soon change, and quickly fail; but Christ remaineth for ever,[2] and standeth by us firmly unto the end.

3. There is no great trust to be put in a frail and mortal man,[3] even though he be profitable and dear unto us : neither ought we to be much grieved, if sometimes he cross and contradict us.

They that to-day take thy part, to-morrow may be against thee ; and often do men turn like the wind.

Put all thy trust in God,[4] let him be thy fear and thy love : he shall answer for thee, and will do all things well, and as is best for thee.

Thou hast not here an abiding city ; [5] and wheresoever thou mayest be, thou art a stranger and pilgrim : neither shalt thou ever have rest, unless thou be inwardly united unto Christ.

4. Why dost thou here gaze about, since this is not the place of thy rest ? In heaven ought to be

[1] John xiv. [23].   [2] John xii. [34].   [3] Jer. xvii. [5].
[4] I Peter v. [7].   [5] Heb. xiii. [14].

thy home,[1] and all earthly things are to be looked upon as it were by the way.

All things pass away,[2] and thou together with them.

Beware thou cleave not unto them, lest thou be caught, and so perish. Let thy thoughts be on the Highest, and thy prayers for mercy directed unto Christ without ceasing.

If thou canst not contemplate high and heavenly things, rest thyself in the passion of Christ and dwell willingly on his sacred wounds.

For if thou fly devoutly unto the wounds and precious marks of the Lord JESUS, thou shalt feel great comfort in tribulation : neither wilt thou much care for the slights of men, and wilt easily bear the words of those that reproach thee.

5. Christ was also in the world despised of men, and in his greatest necessity forsaken by his acquaintance and friends, in the midst of reproaches.[3]

Christ was willing to suffer and be despised ; and darest thou complain of anything ?

Christ had adversaries and backbiters ; and dost thou wish to have all men thy friends and benefactors ?

Whence shall thy patience attain her crown,[4] if no adversity befall thee ?

If thou art willing to suffer no contradiction, how wilt thou be the friend of Christ ?

Suffer with Christ, and for Christ, if thou desire to reign with Christ.

6. If thou hadst but once perfectly entered into

---

[1] Phil. iii. [20].   [2] Wisd. v. [9].
[3] Matt. xii. [24], xvi. [21]; John xx. [20].   [4] 2 Tim. ii. [5].

the secrets of the Lord JESUS, and tasted a little
of his ardent love, then wouldst thou not regard
thine own convenience or inconvenience, but rather
wouldst rejoice in reproaches, if they should be cast
upon thee ; for the love of JESUS maketh a man to
despise himself.

A lover of JESUS and of the truth, and a true
inward Christian, and one free from inordinate affections, can freely turn himself unto God, and lift
himself above himself in spirit, and rest in full
enjoyment.

7. He that judgeth of all things as they are, and
not as they are said or esteemed to be, is truly wise,
and taught rather of God than of men.[1]

He that knoweth how to live inwardly, and to
make small reckoning of things without, neither
requireth places nor awaiteth times for performing
of religious exercises.

A spiritual man quickly recollecteth himself, because he never poureth out himself wholly to outward things.

He is not hindered by outward labour or business,
which may be necessary for the time ; but as things
fall out, so he suits himself to them.

He that is well ordered and disposed within
himself, careth not for the strange and perverse
behaviour of men.

A man is hindered and distracted in proportion as
he draweth outward things unto himself.

8. If it were well with thee, and thou wert
thoroughly purified from sin, all things would fall
out to thee for good,[2] and to thy progress.

---

[1] Isa. liv. [13].   [2] Rom. viii. [28].

But many things displease and often trouble thee, because thou art not yet perfectly dead unto thyself, nor separated from all earthly things.

Nothing so defileth and entangleth the heart of man as the impure love of things created.

If thou refuse outward comfort, thou wilt be able to contemplate the things of heaven, and often to receive internal joy.

CHAPTER II.

Of Humble Submission.

REGARD not much who is for thee, or who against thee;[1] but give all thy thought and care to this, that God be with thee in every thing thou doest.

Have a good conscience, and God will well defend thee.[2]

For whom God will help, no malice of man shall be able to hurt.

If thou canst be silent and suffer, without doubt thou shalt see that the Lord will help thee.

He knoweth the time and the manner to deliver thee, and therefore thou oughtest to resign thyself unto him.

It belongeth to God to help, and to deliver from all confusion.

It is often very profitable, to keep us more humble, that others know and rebuke our faults.

[1] Rom. vii. [31]; 1 Cor. iv. [3].   [2] Ps. xxviii. [7].

2. When a man humbleth himself for his failings, then he easily pacifieth others, and quickly satisfieth those that are offended with him.

God protecteth the humble and delivereth him ; [1] the humble he loveth and comforteth ; unto the humble man he inclineth himself ; unto the humble he giveth great grace ; and after his humiliation he raiseth him to glory.

Unto the humble he revealeth his secrets, [2] and sweetly draweth and inviteth him unto himself.

The humble man, though he suffer confusion, hath yet much peace ; for that he resteth on God, and not on the world.

Do not think that thou hast made any progress, unless thou esteem thyself inferior to all.

CHAPTER III.

Of a Good and Peaceable Man.

FIRST, keep thyself in peace, and then shalt thou be able to make peace among others.

A peaceable man doth more good than he that is well learned.

A passionate man draweth even good into evil, and easily believeth the worst.

A good and peaceable man turneth all things to good.

He that is in peace is not suspicious of any. [3]   But

---

[1] James iii. ; Job v. [11].   [2] Matt. xi. [25].
[3] 1 Cor. xiii. [5].

he that is discontented and troubled is tossed with divers suspicions : he is neither quiet himself, nor suffereth others to be quiet.

He often speaketh that which he ought not to speak, and leaveth undone that which it were more expedient for him to do.

He considereth what others are bound to do,[1] and neglecteth that which he is bound to do himself.

First, therefore, have a careful zeal over thyself,[2] and then thou mayest justly show thyself zealous also of thy neighbour's good.

2. Thou knowest well how to excuse and colour thine own deeds, but thou art not willing to receive the excuses of others.

It were more just that thou shouldst accuse thyself, and excuse thy brother.

If thou wilt thyself be borne with, bear also with another.[3]

Behold, how far off thou art yet from true charity and humility ; for that knows not how to be angry with any, or to be moved with indignation, but only against a man's self.

It is no great matter to associate with the good and gentle ; for this is naturally pleasing to all, and every one willingly enjoyeth peace, and loveth those best that agree with him.

But to be able to live peaceably with hard and perverse persons, or with the disorderly, or with such as go contrary to us, is a great grace, and a most commendable and manly thing.

---

[1] Matt. vii. [3]. [2] Acts xxii. [3].
[3] Gal. vi. [2] ; i Cor. xiii. [7].

3. Some there are that keep themselves in peace, and are in peace also with others.

And there are some that neither are in peace themselves, nor suffer others to be in peace : they are troublesome to others, but always more troublesome to themselves.

And others there are that keep themselves in peace, and study to bring back others unto peace.

Nevertheless, our whole peace in this miserable life consisteth rather in humble endurance, than in not suffering things that are contrary to us.

He that knoweth best how to suffer, will best keep himself in peace. That man is conqueror of himself, and lord of the world, the friend of Christ, and an heir of heaven.

CHAPTER IV.

Of a Pure Mind, and a Simple Intention.

By two wings a man is lifted up from things earthly —namely, by Simplicity and Purity.

Simplicity ought to be in our intention ; purity in our affections. Simplicity doth tend towards God ; purity doth apprehend and taste him.

No good action will hinder thee, if thou be in thy heart free from inordinate affection.

If thou intend and seek nothing else but the will of God and the good of thy neighbour, thou shalt thoroughly enjoy inward liberty.

If thy heart were sincere and upright, then every

creature would be unto thee a living mirror, and a book of holy doctrine.

There is no creature so small and abject, that it representeth not the goodness of God.[1]

2. If thou wert inwardly good and pure,[2] then wouldst thou be able to see and understand all things well without impediment.

A pure heart penetrateth heaven and hell.

Such as every one is inwardly, so he judgeth outwardly.

If there be joy in the world, surely a man of a pure heart possesseth it.

And if there be anywhere tribulation and affliction, an evil conscience best knoweth it.

As iron put into the fire loseth its rust, and becometh clearly red hot, so he that wholly turneth himself unto God, putteth off all slothfulness, and is transformed into a new man.

3. When a man beginneth to grow lukewarm, then he is afraid of a little labour, and willingly receiveth comfort from outward things.

But when he once beginneth to overcome himself perfectly, and to walk manfully in the way of God, then he esteemeth those things to be light which before seemed grievous unto him.

[1] Rom. i. [20].   [2] Prov. iii. [3, 4]; Ps. cxix. [100].

CHAPTER V.

Of the Consideration of One's Self.

WE cannot trust much to ourselves,[1] because grace oftentimes is wanting to us, and understanding also.

There is but little light in us, and that which we have we quickly lose by our negligence.

Oftentimes too we do not perceive our own inward blindness how great it is.

We often do a bad act, and make a worse excuse.[2]

We are sometimes moved with passion, and we think it to be zeal.

We reprehend small things in others, and pass over greater matters in ourselves.[3]

We quickly enough feel and weigh what we suffer at the hands of others; but we mind not what others suffer from us.

He that well and rightly considereth his own works, will find little cause to judge hardly of another.

2. He who is a Christian at heart preferreth the care of himself before all other cares.[4] And he that diligently attendeth unto himself, can easily keep silence concerning others.

Thou wilt never be thus in heart religious, unless thou pass over other men's matters with silence, and look especially to thyself.

If thou attend wholly unto God and thyself, thou wilt be but little moved with whatsoever thou seest abroad.[5]

---

[1] Jer. xvii. [5].   [2] Ps. cxli. [4].   [3] Matt. vii. [5].
[4] Matt. xvi. [26].   [5] 1 Cor. iv. [3]; Gal. i. [10].

Where art thou, when thou art not with thyself? And when thou hast run over all, what hast thou then profited, if thou hast neglected thyself?

If thou desirest peace of mind and true unity of purpose, thou must still put all other things behind thee, and look only upon thyself.

3. Thou shalt profit much if thou keep thyself free from all temporal care.

Thou shalt greatly lose if thou take thought for any temporal thing.

Let nothing be great unto thee, nothing high, nothing pleasing, nothing acceptable, but only God himself, or that which is of God.

Esteem all comfort vain [1] which thou receivest from any creature.

A soul that loveth God, despiseth all things that are inferior unto God.

God alone is everlasting, and of infinite greatness, filling all creatures; the comfort of the soul, and the true joy of the heart.

CHAPTER VI.

Of the Joy of a Good Conscience.

THE glory of a good man is the testimony of a good conscience. [2]

Have a good conscience, and thou shalt ever have joy.

[1] Eccles. i. [14].   [2] 1 Cor. i. [31].

A good conscience is able to bear very much, and is very cheerful in adversities.

An evil conscience is always fearful and unquiet.[1]

Thou shalt rest sweetly if thy heart condemn thee not.

Never rejoice but when thou hast done well.

Sinners have never true joy, nor feel inward peace ; because " There is no peace to the wicked," saith the Lord.[2]

And if they should say, " We are in peace, no evil shall fall upon us,[3] and who shall dare to hurt us ? " believe them not ; for upon a sudden will arise the wrath of God, and their deeds shall be brought to nought, and their thoughts shall perish.

2. To glory in tribulation is no hard thing for him that loveth ; for so to glory, is to glory in the cross of the Lord.[4]

That glory is short which is given and received from men.[5]

Sorrow always accompanieth the glory of the world.

The glory of the good is in their consciences, and not in the tongues of men. The gladness of the just is of God,[6] and in God ; and their joy is of the truth.

He that desireth true and everlasting glory, careth not for that which is temporal.

And he that seeketh temporal glory, or despiseth it not from his soul, showeth himself to have but little esteem of the glory of heaven.

[1] Wisd. xvii. [11].   [2] Isa. lvii. [21].   [3] Luke xii. [19].
[4] Rom. viii. ; Gal. vi. [14].   [5] John v. [44].   [6] 2 Cor. iii. [5].

He enjoyeth great tranquillity of heart that careth neither for the praise nor dispraise of men.

3. He will easily be content and at peace whose conscience is pure.

Thou art not the more holy for being praised, nor the more worthless for being dispraised.

What thou art, that thou art ; neither by words canst thou be made greater than what thou art in the sight of God.

If thou consider what thou art in thyself, thou wilt not care what men say of thee.

Man looketh on the countenance, but God on the heart.[1] Man considereth the deeds, but God weigheth the intentions.

To be always doing good, and to esteem little of one's self, is the sign of an humble soul.

To be unwilling to have any created being for our comforter, is a sign of great purity and inward confidence.

4. He that seeketh no testimony on his behalf from without, doth show that he hath wholly committed himself unto God.

"For not he that commendeth himself is approved," saith Saint Paul, "but whom God commendeth." [2]

To walk in the heart with God, and not to be held in bondage by any outward affection, is the state of a spiritual man.

[1] 1 Sam. xvi. [7].　　[2] 2 Cor. x. [18].

CHAPTER VII.

Of the Love of Jesus above all Things.

BLESSED is he that understandeth [1] what it is to love JESUS, and to despise himself for JESUS' sake.

Thou oughtest to leave thy beloved for the Beloved; [2] for JESUS will be loved alone above all things.

The love of things created is deceitful and inconstant; the love of JESUS is faithful and constant.

He that cleaveth unto creatures shall fall with that which is subject to fall; he that embraceth JESUS shall stand firmly for ever.

Love him, and keep him for thy friend, who, when all go away, will not forsake thee, nor suffer thee to perish in the end.

Some time or other thou must be separated from all, whether thou wilt or no.

2. Keep close to JESUS both in life and in death, and commit thyself unto his faithfulness, who, when all fail, can alone help thee.

Thy Beloved is of such a nature that he will admit of no rival, but will have thy heart alone, and sit on his own throne as King.

If thou couldst empty thyself perfectly of all created things, JESUS would willingly dwell with thee.

Whatsoever trust thou reposest in men, out of JESUS, is all little better than lost.

Trust not nor lean upon a reed shaken by the

---

[1] Ps. cxix. [1, 2].
[2] Deut. vi. [5]; Song of Sol. ii. [16]; Matt. xxii. [37].

wind ; for that all flesh is grass, and all the glory thereof shall wither away as the flower of the field.[1]

3. Thou wilt soon be deceived, if thou only look to the outward appearance of men.

For if thou seekest thy comfort and thy profit in others, thou shalt often feel loss.

If thou seekest Jesus in all things, thou shalt surely find Jesus.

But if thou seekest thyself, thou shalt also find thyself, but to thine own destruction.

For if a man do not seek Jesus, he is more hurtful to himself than the whole world and all his enemies could be.

CHAPTER VIII.

Of Familiar Friendship with Jesus.

When Jesus is present, all is well, and nothing seems difficult ; but when Jesus is not present, everything is hard.

When Jesus speaks not inwardly to us, all other comfort is nothing worth ; but if Jesus speak but one word, we feel great consolation.

Did not Mary rise immediately from the place where she wept when Martha said to her, " The Master is come, and calleth for thee " ? [2]

Happy hour ! when Jesus calleth from tears to spiritual joy.

[1] Isa. xl. [6].   [2] John xi. [28].

How dry and hard art thou without JESUS! How foolish and vain, if thou desire anything out of JESUS!

Is not this a greater loss than if thou shouldst lose the whole world? [1]

2. What can the world profit thee without JESUS?

To be without JESUS is a grievous hell, and to be with JESUS a sweet paradise.

If JESUS be with thee, no enemy shall be able to hurt thee.[2]

He that findeth JESUS findeth a good treasure,[3] yea, a good above all good.

And he that loseth JESUS loseth overmuch, yea, more than the whole world!

Most poor is he who liveth without JESUS; [4] and he most rich who is dear to JESUS.

3. It asketh great skill to know how to hold converse with JESUS; and to know how to retain JESUS is great wisdom.

Be thou humble and peaceable, and JESUS will be with thee.[5]

Be devout and quiet, and JESUS will stay with thee.

Thou mayest soon drive away JESUS, and lose his favour, if thou wilt turn aside to outward things.

And if thou shouldst drive him from thee and lose him, unto whom wilt thou flee, and whom wilt thou then seek for thy friend?

Without a friend thou canst not well live; and it JESUS be not above all friends to thee, thou shalt be indeed sad and desolate.

[1] Matt. xvi. [26].   [2] Rom. viii. [35].   [3] Matt. xiii. [44].
[4] Luke xii. [21].   [5] Prov. iii. [17].

Therefore thou doest not wisely if thou trust or rejoice in any other.[1]

It is preferable to have all the world against us, rather than to have JESUS offended with us.

Amongst all therefore that be dear unto us, let JESUS alone be specially beloved.

4. Love all for JESUS, but JESUS for himself.

JESUS Christ alone is singularly to be loved; and he alone is found good and faithful above all friends.

For him, and in him, let friends as well as foes be dear unto thee; and all these are to be prayed for, that he would make them all to know and to love him.[2]

Never desire to be singularly commended or beloved, for that appertaineth only unto God, who hath none like unto himself.

Neither do thou desire that the heart of any should be set on thee, nor do thou set thy heart on the love of any; but let JESUS be in thee, and in every good man.

5. Be pure and free within, and entangle not thy heart with any creature.

Thou oughtest to be naked and open before God, ever carrying thy heart pure towards him, if thou wouldst be free to consider and see how sweet the Lord is.

And truly, unless thou be prevented and drawn by his grace, thou shalt never attain to that happiness of forsaking and taking leave of all, in order that thou alone mayest be united to him alone.

For when the grace of God cometh unto a man,

[1] Gal. vi. [14].   [2] Matt. v. [44]; Luke vi. [27, 28].

then he is made able for all things. And when it goeth away, then is he poor and weak, and as it were left only for affliction.

In this case thou oughtest not to be cast down, nor to despair ; but to resign thyself calmly to the will of God, and whatever comes upon thee, to endure it for the glory of JESUS Christ ; for after winter followeth summer, after night the day returneth, and after a tempest a great calm.

CHAPTER IX.

Of the Want of all Comfort.

IT is no hard matter to despise human comfort [1] when we have that which is divine.

It is much and very much to be able to lack both human and divine comfort; and, for God's honour, to be willing cheerfully to endure desolation of heart ; and to seek oneself in nothing, nor to regard one's own merit.

What great matter is it, if at the coming of grace thou be cheerful and devout ? this hour is wished for of all men.

He rideth easily enough whom the grace of God carrieth.

And what marvel if he feel not his burden who is borne up by the Almighty, and led by the Sovereign Guide ?

2. We are always willing to have something for

[1] Phil. ii. [12].

our comfort ; and a man doth not without difficulty
strip himself of self.

The holy martyr Laurence and his priest overcame the world, because whatsoever seemed de-
lightsome in the world he despised ; and for the
love of Christ he patiently suffered God's chief
priest Sixtus, whom he most dearly loved, to be
even taken away from him.

He therefore overcame the love of man by the
love of the Creator ; and he rather chose what
pleased God than human comfort.

So also do thou learn to part even with a near
and dear friend for the love of God.

Nor do thou think it hard, when thou art deserted
by a friend, as knowing that we all at last must
be separated one from another.

3. A man must strive long and mightily within
himself before he can learn fully to master himself,
and to draw his whole heart unto God.

When a man trusteth in himself, he easily slideth
unto human comforts.

But a true lover of Christ, and a diligent follower
of all virtue, does not fall back on comforts, nor
seek such sensible sweetnesses ; but rather prefers
hard exercises, and to sustain severe labours for
Christ.

4. When therefore spiritual comfort is given
thee from God, receive it with thankfulness ; but
understand that it is the gift of God, not thy
desert.

Be not puffed up, be not too joyful, nor vainly
presumptuous ; but rather be the more humble for
that gift, more wary too and fearful in all thine

actions ; for that hour will pass away, and temptation will follow.

When consolation is taken from thee, do not immediately despair ; but with humility and patience wait for the heavenly visitation ; for God is able to give thee back again more ample consolation.

This is nothing new nor strange unto them that have experience in the way of God ; for the great saints and ancient prophets had oftentimes experience of such kind of vicissitudes.

5. For which cause, one, while he was basking in divine grace, said, " I said in my prosperity, I shall never be moved." [1]

But in the absence of it, he adds this experience of what he was in himself, " Thou didst turn thy face from me, and I was troubled."

Yet in the midst of all this he doth not by any means despair, but more earnestly beseecheth the Lord, and saith, " Unto thee, O Lord, will I cry, and I will pray unto my God."

At length he receiveth the fruit of his prayer, and testifieth that he was heard, saying, " The Lord hath heard me, and taken pity on me ; the Lord is become my helper."

But wherein ? " Thou hast turned," saith he, " my sorrow into joy, and thou hast compassed me about with gladness."

If great saints were so dealt with, we that are weak and poor ought not to despair if we be sometimes hot and sometimes cold ; for the Spirit cometh and goeth according to the good pleasure of his own will.[2] For which cause holy Job saith,

[1] Ps. xxx. [6-11].   [2] John iii. [8].

" Thou visitest him early in the morning, and suddenly thou provest him." [1]

6. Whereupon then can I hope, or wherein ought I to trust, save in the great mercy of God alone, and in the only hope of heavenly grace ?

For whether I have with me good men, either religious brethren, or faithful friends ; whether holy books, or beautiful treatises, or sweet psalms and hymns ; all these help but little, and have but little savour, when grace forsaketh me, and I am left in mine own poverty.

At such time there is no better remedy than patience, and the denying of myself according to the will of God.[2]

7. I never found any so religious and devout that he had not sometimes a withdrawing of grace, or felt not some decrease of zeal.

There was never saint so highly rapt and illuminated who first or last was not tempted.

For he is not worthy of the high contemplation of God who hath not been exercised with some tribulation for God's sake.

For temptation going before is wont to be a sign of comfort to follow.

For unto those that are proved by temptations heavenly comfort is promised. " To him that overcometh," saith He, " I will give to eat of the tree of life." [3]

8. But divine consolation is given, that a man may be stronger to bear adversities.

There followeth also temptation, lest he should wax proud of any good.

[1] Job vii. [18].   [2] Luke ix. [23].   [3] Rev. ii. [7].

The devil sleepeth not,[1] neither is the flesh as yet dead ; therefore cease not to prepare thyself to the battle ; for on thy right hand and on thy left are enemies who never rest.

CHAPTER X.

Of Gratitude for the Grace of God.

WHY seekest thou rest, since thou art born to labour ?[2]

Dispose thyself to patience rather than to comfort, and to the bearing of the cross rather than to gladness.[3]

What worldly man is there that would not willingly receive spiritual joy and comfort if he could always have it ?

For spiritual comforts exceed all the delights of the world, and the pleasures of the flesh.

For all worldly delights are either vain or unclean ; but spiritual delights alone are pleasant and honest, being sprung from virtue, and infused by God into pure minds.

But no man can always enjoy these divine comforts according to his desire ; for the time of temptation is never far away.

2. But false freedom of mind and great confidence in ourselves are very contrary to heavenly visitations.

God doeth well for us in giving the grace of com-

[1] 1 Peter v. [8].   [2] Job v. [7].   [3] Luke xiv. [27].

fort ; but man doeth evil in not returning all again unto God with thanksgiving.

And therefore the gifts of grace cannot flow in us, because we are unthankful to the giver, and return them not wholly to the source and fountain.[1]

For grace ever attendeth him that is duly thankful ; and from the proud shall be taken that which is wont to be given to the humble.

3. I desire not that consolation that taketh from me compunction ; nor do I affect that contemplation which leadeth to a high mind.

For all that is high is not holy ; nor all that is sweet, good ; nor every desire, pure ; nor is every thing that is dear unto us pleasing to God.

Willingly do I accept of that grace, whereby I may ever be found more humble, and more affected with fear, and may become more ready to renounce myself.

He that is taught by the gift of grace, and schooled by the withdrawing thereof, will not dare to attribute any good to himself, but will rather acknowledge himself to be poor and naked.

Give unto God that which is God's,[2] and ascribe unto thyself that which is thine own—that is, give thanks to God for his grace ; and acknowledge that to thyself alone is to be attributed sin, and the punishment due to sin.

4. Set thyself always in the lowest place,[3] and the highest shall be given thee ; for the highest is not without the lowest.

The chiefest saints before God are the least in their own judgments ; and the more glorious they are, so much the humbler within themselves.

[1] Ecclus. i. [5].   [2] Matt. xxii. [21].   [3] Luke xiv. [10].

Those that are full of truth and heavenly glory are not desirous of empty glory.

Those that are firmly settled and grounded in God can in no way be proud.

And they that ascribe all good unto God, whatsoever they have received, seek not glory one of another, but desire that glory which is from God alone ; and above all things that God may be praised in himself, and in all his saints ; and are always pressing on for this very thing.

5. Be therefore thankful for the least gift, so shalt thou be meet to receive greater.

Let the least be unto thee even as the greatest, yea the most contemptible gift as of especial value.

If thou consider the worth of the Giver, no gift will seem little, or of too mean esteem. For that cannot be little which is given by the most High God.

Yea, if he should give punishment and stripes, it ought to be matter of thankfulness ; because he doeth always for our welfare whatsoever he permitteth to happen unto us.

He that desireth to keep the grace of God, let him be thankful for grace given, and patient for the taking away thereof : let him pray that it may return ; let him be cautious and humble, lest he lose it.

CHAPTER XI.

That the Lovers of the Cross of Jesus are Few.

JESUS hath now many lovers of his heavenly kingdom, but few bearers of his cross.

He hath many desirous of consolation, but few of tribulation.

He findeth many companions of his table, but few of his abstinence.

All desire to rejoice with him, few are willing to endure anything for him.

Many follow JESUS unto the breaking of bread, but few to the drinking of the cup of his passion.[1]

Many reverence his miracles, few follow the ignominy of his cross.

Many love JESUS so long as no adversities befall them.

Many praise and bless him so long as they receive any consolation from him.

But if JESUS hide himself, and leave them but a little while, they fall either into complaining, or into too much dejection of mind.

2. But they who love JESUS for his own sake, and not for some special comfort which they receive, bless him in all tribulation and anguish of heart, as well as in the state of highest comfort.

Yea, although he should never be willing to give them comfort, they notwithstanding would ever praise him, and wish to be always giving thanks.

3. Oh how powerful is the pure love of JESUS, which is mixed with no self-interest, nor self-love !

[1] Luke ix. [14], xxii. [41, 42].

Are not all those to be called mercenary who are ever seeking consolations ?

Do they not show themselves to be rather lovers of themselves than of Christ, who are always thinking of their own profit and advantage ? [1]

Where shall one be found who is willing to serve God for nought ?

4. Rarely is any one found so spiritual as to have suffered the loss of all things.

For where is any man to be found that is indeed poor in spirit, and thoroughly void of all leaning on created things ? " From afar, yea from the ends of the earth, is his value." [2]

If a man should give all his substance, it is as yet nothing.

And if he should practise great repentance, still it is little.

And if he should attain to all knowledge, he is still afar off.

And if he should be of great virtue, and of very fervent devotion, yet there is much wanting : especially one thing, which is most necessary for him.

What is that ? That leaving all, he forsake himself, and go wholly from himself,[3] and retain nothing of self-love.

And when he hath done all that is to be done, so far as he knoweth, let him think that he hath done nothing.

5. Let him not think that of great weight which might be esteemed great ; but let him in truth pronounce himself to be an unprofitable servant, as the Truth himself saith, " When you shall have done

[1] Phil. ii. [21].   [2] Prov. xxxi. [10, Latin version].   [3] Matt. xvi. [24].

all things that are commanded you, say, We are unprofitable servants." [1]

Then may he be truly poor and naked in spirit, and say with the prophet, " I am desolate and afflicted." [2]

Yet none is richer than that man, none more powerful, none more free ; for he knoweth how to leave himself and all things, and to set himself in the lowest place

CHAPTER XII.

Of the Royal Way of the Holy Cross.

UNTO many this seemeth an hard speech, " Deny thyself, take up thy cross, and follow JESUS." [3]

But much harder will it be to hear that last word, " Depart from me, ye cursed, into everlasting fire." [4]

For they who now willingly hear and follow the word of the cross shall not then fear [5] to hear the sentence of everlasting damnation.

This sign of the cross shall be in the heaven when the Lord shall come to judgment.

Then all the servants of the cross, who in their life-time conformed themselves unto Christ crucified, shall draw near unto Christ the judge with great confidence.

2. Why therefore fearest thou to take up the cross which leadeth thee to a kingdom ?

In the cross is salvation, in the cross is life, in the cross is protection against our enemies, in the cross

[1] Luke xvii. [10].   [2] Ps. xxv. [16].   [3] Matt. xvi. [24].
[4] Matt. xxv. [41].   [5] Ps. cxii. [7].

is infusion of heavenly sweetness, in the cross is strength of mind, in the cross joy of spirit, in the cross the height of virtue, in the cross the perfection of sanctity.

There is no salvation of the soul, nor hope of everlasting life, but in the cross.

Take up therefore thy cross and follow JESUS,[1] and thou shalt go into life everlasting. He went before, bearing his cross,[2] and died for thee on the cross, that thou mightest also bear thy cross and desire to die on the cross with him.

For if thou be dead with him, thou shalt also live with him. And if thou be his companion in punishment, thou shalt be partaker with him also in glory.[3]

3. Behold! in the cross all doth consist, and all lieth in our dying thereon; for there is no other way unto life, and unto true inward peace, but the way of the holy cross, and of daily mortification.

Go where thou wilt, seek whatsoever thou wilt, thou shalt not find a higher way above, nor a safer way below, than the way of the holy cross.

Dispose and order all things according to thy will and judgment; yet thou shalt ever find, that of necessity thou must suffer somewhat, either willingly or against thy will, and so thou shalt ever find the cross.

For either thou shalt feel pain in thy body, or in thy soul thou shalt suffer tribulation.

4. Sometimes thou shalt be forsaken of God, sometimes thou shalt be troubled by thy neighbours; and what is more, oftentimes thou shalt be wearisome to thyself.

[1] Luke xiv. [27].   [2] John xix. [17].   [3] 2 Cor. i. [5].

Neither canst thou be delivered or eased by any remedy or comfort ; but so long as it pleaseth God, thou must bear it.

For God will have thee learn to suffer tribulation without comfort ; and that thou subject thyself wholly to him, and by tribulation become more humble.

No man hath so in his heart a sympathy with the passion of Christ, as he who hath suffered the like himself.

The cross therefore is always ready, and everywhere waits for thee.

Thou canst not escape it whithersoever thou runnest ; for wheresoever thou goest, thou carriest thyself with thee, and shalt ever find thyself.

Both above and below, without and within, which way soever thou dost turn thee, everywhere thou shalt find the cross ; and everywhere of necessity thou must hold fast patience, if thou wilt have inward peace and enjoy an everlasting crown.

5. If thou bear the cross cheerfully, it will bear thee, and lead thee to the desired end—namely, where there shall be an end of suffering, though here there shall not be.

If thou bear it unwillingly, thou makest for thyself a burden, and increasest thy load, which yet notwithstanding thou must bear.

If thou cast away one cross, without doubt thou shalt find another, and that perhaps more heavy.

6. Thinkest thou to escape that which no mortal man could ever avoid ? Which of the saints in the world was without crosses and tribulation ?

For not even our Lord JESUS Christ was ever one

hour without the anguish of his passion, so long as he lived. " Christ," saith he, " must needs suffer, and rise again from the dead, and so enter into his glory." [1] And how dost thou seek any other way than this royal way, which is the way of the holy cross?

7. Christ's whole life was a cross and martyrdom: and dost thou seek rest and joy for thyself?

Thou art deceived, thou art deceived if thou seek any other thing than to suffer tribulations; for this whole mortal life is full of miseries, [2] and marked on every side with crosses.

And the higher a person hath advanced in the Spirit, so much the heavier crosses he oftentimes findeth; because the grief of his banishment increaseth with his love to God.

8. Nevertheless this man, though so many ways afflicted, is not without refreshing comfort, for that he perceiveth very much benefit to accrue unto him by the bearing of his own cross.

For whilst he willingly putteth himself under it, all the burden of tribulation is turned into the confidence of divine comfort.

And the more the flesh is wasted by affliction, so much the more is the spirit strengthened by inward grace.

And sometimes he is so comforted with the desire of tribulation and adversity, for the love of conformity to the cross of Christ, that he would not wish to be without grief and tribulation; [3] because he believes that he shall be unto God so much the more acceptable, the more and the more grievous things he is permitted to suffer for him.

[1] Luke xxiv. [26].   [2] Job vii. [1].   [3] 2 Cor. iv. [16], xi. [23–30].

This is not the power of man, but it is the grace of Christ, which can and doth so much in frail flesh; so that what naturally it always abhors and flees from, that through fervour of spirit it encounters and loves.

9. It is not according to man's inclination to bear the cross, to love the cross, to chastise the body and bring it into subjection, to flee honours, willingly to suffer contumelies, to despise oneself and to wish to be despised, to endure all adversities and losses, and to desire no prosperity in this world.

If thou look to thyself, thou shalt be able of thyself to accomplish nothing of this kind.[1]

But if thou trust in the Lord, strength shall be given thee from heaven, and the world and the flesh shall be made subject to thy command.

Neither shalt thou fear thine enemy the devil, if thou be armed with faith, and signed with the cross of Christ.

10. Set thyself, therefore, like a good and faithful servant of Christ, to bear manfully the cross of thy Lord, who out of love was crucified for thee.

Prepare thyself to bear many adversities and divers kinds of troubles in this miserable life; for so it will be with thee, wheresoever thou art, and so surely thou shalt find it, wheresoever thou hide thyself.

So it must be; nor is there any remedy nor means to escape from tribulation and sorrow, but only to endure them.

Drink of the Lord's cup [2] with hearty affection, if

[1] 2 Cor. iii. [5].   [2] Matt. xx. [23]; John xviii. [11].

thou desire to be his friend, and to have part with him.

As for comforts, leave them to God; let him do therein as shall best please him.

But do thou set thyself to suffer tribulations, and account them the greatest comforts; for the sufferings of this present time, although thou alone couldst suffer them all, cannot worthily deserve the glory which is to come.

11. When thou shalt come to this estate, that tribulation [1] shall seem sweet, and thou shalt relish it for Christ's sake, then think it to be well with thee, for thou hast found a paradise upon earth.

As long as it is grievous to thee to suffer, and thou desirest to escape, so long shalt thou be ill at ease, and the desire of escaping tribulation shall follow thee everywhere.

12. If thou dost set thyself to that thou oughtest —namely, to suffering and to death—it will quickly be better with thee, and thou shalt find peace.

Although thou shouldst have been rapt even unto the third heaven with Paul,[2] thou art not by this secured that thou shalt suffer no adversity. " I will show him," saith JESUS, " how great things he must suffer for my name." [3]

It remaineth therefore that thou suffer, if it please thee to love JESUS, and to serve him constantly.

13. Oh that thou wert worthy to suffer something for the name of JESUS! [4] How great glory would remain unto thyself; what joy would arise

---

[1] Rom. v. [3]; Gal. vi. [14].   [2] 2 Cor. xii. [4].
[3] Acts ix. [16].   [4] Acts v. [41].

to all God's saints; how great edification also to thy neighbour!

For all men recommend patience; few, however, they are who are willing to suffer.

With great reason oughtest thou cheerfully to suffer some little for Christ's sake, since many suffer more grievous things for the world.

14. Know for certain that thou oughtest to lead a dying life.[1] And the more any man dieth to himself, so much the more doth he begin to live unto God.

No man is fit to comprehend things heavenly, unless he submit himself to the bearing of adversities for Christ's sake.

Nothing is more acceptable to God, nothing more wholesome to thee in this world, than that thou suffer cheerfully for Christ.

And if thou couldst choose, thou oughtest rather to wish to suffer adversities for Christ, than to be refreshed with many consolations; because thou wouldst thus be more like unto Christ, and more conformable to all the saints.

For our worthiness and the growth of our spiritual estate consisteth not in many sweetnesses and comforts, but rather in the patient enduring of great afflictions and tribulations.

15. Indeed if there had been any better thing, and more profitable to man's salvation, than suffering, surely Christ would have showed it by word and example

For both the disciples that followed him, and also all who desire to follow him, he plainly exhorteth to

[1] Ps. xliv. [22].

the bearing of the cross, and saith, " If any man will come after me, let him deny himself, and take up his cross, and follow me." [1]

So that when we have thoroughly read and searched all, let this be the final conclusion, " That through much tribulation we must enter into the kingdom of God." [2]

[1] Luke ix. [23].   [2] Acts xiv. [22].

THE THIRD BOOK.
OF INTERNAL CONSOLATION.

THE THIRD BOOK.

CHAPTER I.

Of Christ's Speaking inwardly to the Faithful Soul.

I WILL hearken what the Lord God will speak in me.[1]

Blessed is the soul which heareth the Lord speaking within her,[2] and receiveth from his mouth the word of consolation.

Blessed are the ears that gladly receive the pulses of the Divine whisper,[3] and give no heed to the many whisperings of this world.

Blessed indeed are those ears which listen not after the voice which is sounding without, but for the Truth teaching within.

Blessed are the eyes which are shut to outward things, but intent on things within.

Blessed are they that enter far into inward things, and endeavour to prepare themselves, more and more, by daily exercises, for the receiving of heavenly secrets.

[1] Ps. lxxxv. [8].   [2] I Sam. iii. [9].   [3] Matt. xiii. [16, 17].

Blessed are they who are glad to have time to spare for God, and who shake off all worldly hindrances.

2. Consider these things, O my soul, and shut up the door of thy sensual desires, that thou mayest hear what the Lord thy God shall speak in thee.[1]

Thus saith thy Beloved, I am thy Salvation,[2] thy Peace, and thy Life : keep thyself with me, and thou shalt find peace.

Let go all transitory things, and seek those that be everlasting.

What are all temporal things but snares ? and what can all creatures avail thee, if thou be forsaken by the Creator ?

Bid farewell therefore to all things else, and labour to please thy Creator, and to be faithful unto him, that so thou mayest be able to attain unto true blessedness.

CHAPTER II.

That the Truth Speaketh inwardly without Noise of Words.

Speak, Lord, for thy servant heareth.[3]

I am thy servant, grant me understanding, that I may know thy testimonies.[4]

Incline my heart to the words of thy mouth : let thy speech distil as the dew.

The children of Israel in times past said unto

---

[1] Ps. lxxxv. [8]. [2] Ps. xxxv. [3].
[3] 1 Sam. iii. [9]. [4] Ps. cxix. [125].

Moses, " Speak thou unto us, and we will hear : let not the Lord speak unto us, lest we die." [1]

Not so, Lord, not so, I beseech thee ; but rather with the prophet Samuel, I humbly and earnestly entreat, " Speak, Lord, for thy servant heareth."

Let not Moses speak unto me, nor any of the prophets, but rather do thou speak, O Lord God, the inspirer and enlightener of all the prophets ; for thou alone without them canst perfectly instruct me, but they without thee can profit nothing.

2. They indeed may utter words, but they cannot give the Spirit.

Most beautifully do they speak, but if thou be silent, they inflame not the heart.

They teach the letter, but thou openest the sense ; they bring forth mysteries, but thou unlockest the meaning of sealed things.

They declare thy commandments, but thou helpest us to fulfil them.

They point out the way, but thou givest strength to walk in it.

They work only outwardly, but thou instructest and enlightenest the heart.

They water, but thou givest the increase.

They cry aloud in words, but thou impartest understanding to the hearing.

3. Let not Moses therefore speak unto me, but thou, O Lord my God, the everlasting Truth ; lest I die, and prove unfruitful, if I be only warned outwardly, and not inflamed within :

Lest it turn to my condemnation,—the word heard

[1] Ex. xx. [19].

and not fulfilled, known and not loved, believed and not observed.

Speak therefore, Lord, for thy servant heareth ; for thou hast the words of eternal life.[1]

Speak thou unto me, to the comfort, however imperfect, of my soul, and to the amendment of my whole life, and to thy praise and glory and honour everlasting.

CHAPTER III.

That the Words of God are to be heard with Humility, and that many weigh them not.

MY son, hear my words, words of greatest sweetness, surpassing all the knowledge of the philosophers and wise men of this world.

"My words are spirit and life,"[2] and not to be weighed by the understanding of man.

They are not to be drawn forth for vain approbation, but to be heard in silence, and to be received with all humility and great affection.

AND I said, Blessed is the man whom thou shalt instruct, O Lord, and shalt teach out of thy law, that thou mayest give him rest from the evil days,[3] and that he be not desolate upon earth.

2. I TAUGHT the prophets from the beginning[4] (saith the Lord), and cease not, even to this day, to

[1] John vi. [68].   [2] John vi. [63].
[3] Ps. xciv. [12, 13].   [4] Heb. i. [1].

speak to all; but many are hardened, and deaf to my voice.

Most men do more willingly listen to the world than to God; they sooner follow the desires of their own flesh than God's good pleasure.

The world promiseth things temporal and mean, and is served with great eagerness; I promise things most high and eternal, and yet the hearts of men remain torpid and insensible.

Who is there that in all things serveth and obeyeth me with so great care as the world and its lords are served withal? Be ashamed, O Sidon, saith the sea.[1] And if thou ask the cause, hear wherefore.

For a small income a long journey is undertaken; for everlasting life many will scarce once lift a foot from the ground.

The most pitiful reward is sought after; for a single bit of money sometimes there is shameful contention; for a vain matter and slight promise men fear not to toil day and night.

3. But, alas! for an unchangeable good, for an inestimable reward, for the highest honour, and glory without end, they grudge even the least fatigue.

Be ashamed, therefore, thou slothful and complaining servant, that they are found to be more ready to destruction than thou to life.

They rejoice more in vanity than thou dost in the truth.

Sometimes, indeed, they are frustrated of their hope; but my promise deceiveth none,[2] nor sendeth him away empty that trusteth in me.

What I have promised, I will give; what I have

[1] Comp. Isa. xxiii. [4].　　[2] Rom. i. [16]; Matt. xxiv. [35].

said, I will fulfil ; if only any man remain faithful in my love even to the end.

I am the rewarder of all good men,[1] and the strong approver of all who are devoted to me.

4. Write thou my words in thy heart, and meditate diligently on them ; for in time of temptation they will be very needful for thee.

What thou understandest not when thou readest, thou shalt know in the day of visitation.

In two ways I am wont to visit mine elect— namely, with temptation and with consolation.

And I daily read two lessons to them, one in reproving their vices, another in exhorting them to the increase of all virtues.

He that hath my words and despiseth them, hath one that shall judge him in the last day.

5. *A Prayer to implore the grace of Devotion.*

O Lord my God ! thou art to me whatsoever is good. And who am I, that I should dare to speak to thee ?[2] I am thy poorest, meanest servant, and a most vile worm, much more poor and contemptible than I can or dare express.

Yet do thou remember, O Lord, that I am nothing, have nothing, and can do nothing.

Thou alone art good, just, and holy ; thou canst do all things, thou accomplishest all things, thou fillest all things, only the sinner thou leavest empty.

Remember thy mercies, and fill my heart with thy grace, thou who wilt not that thy works should be void and in vain.

[1] Rev. ii. [23] ; Matt. v. [6], xxv. [21].
[2] Gen. xviii. [27] ; 1 Sam. xviii. [18, 23].

6. How can I bear up myself in this miserable life, unless thou strengthen me with thy mercy and grace?

Turn not thy face away from me; [1] delay not thy visitation; withdraw not thy consolation, lest my soul become as a thirsty land.

Teach me, O Lord, to do thy will; [2] teach me to live worthily and humbly in thy sight; for thou art my wisdom, thou dost truly know me, and didst know me before the world was made, and before I was born into the world.

CHAPTER IV.

That we ought to live in Truth and Humility before God.

My son, walk thou before me in truth, and ever seek me in simplicity of thy heart. [3]

He that walketh before me in truth, shall be defended from the assaults of evil, and the truth shall set him [4] free from seducers, and from the slanders of unjust men.

If the truth shall have made thee free, thou shalt be free indeed, and shalt not care for the vain words of men.

O Lord, it is true. According as thou sayest, so, I beseech thee, let it be with me; let thy truth teach me, guard me, and preserve me safe to the end.

[1] Ps. lxix. [17].
[2] Ps. cxliii. [10].
[3] Gen. xvii. [1]; Wisd. i. [1].
[4] John viii. [32].

Let it set me free from all evil affection and inordinate love; and I shall walk with thee in great liberty of heart.

2. I WILL teach thee (saith the Truth) those things which are right and pleasing in my sight.

Reflect on thy sins with great displeasure and grief; and never esteem thyself to be anything, because of any good works.

In truth thou art a sinner; thou art subject to and encumbered with many passions. Of thyself thou always tendest to nothing; speedily art thou cast down, speedily overcome, speedily disordered, speedily dissolved.

Thou hast nothing whereof thou canst glory,[1] but many things for which thou oughtest to account thyself vile; for thou art much weaker than thou art able to comprehend.

3. And therefore let nothing seem much unto thee whatsoever thou doest.

Let nothing seem great, nothing precious and wonderful, nothing worthy of estimation, nothing high, nothing truly commendable, and to be desired, but that alone which is eternal.

Let the eternal truth be above all things pleasing to thee: let thine own extreme unworthiness be always displeasing to thee.

Fear nothing, blame nothing, flee nothing, so much as thy vices and sins, which ought to be more unpleasing to thee than any losses whatsoever of things earthly.

Some walk not sincerely in my sight,[2] but out of

[1] 1 Cor. iv. [7].   [2] Ecclus. iii. [21–23]; 2 Cor. ii. [17].

curiosity and pride desire to know my secrets, and to understand the high things of God, neglecting themselves and their own salvation.

These oftentimes when I oppose myself to them, for their pride and curiosity do fall into great temptations and sins.

4. Fear thou the judgments of God, and dread the wrath of the Almighty. Discuss not thou the works of the Most High, but search diligently thine own iniquities, in how great things thou hast offended, and how many good things thou hast neglected.

Some place their devotion only in books, some in pictures, some in outward signs and figures.

Some have me in their mouths, but little in their hearts.[1]

Others there are who, being illuminated in their understandings, and purged in their affection, do always pant after things eternal, are unwilling to hear of the things of this world, and serve the necessities of nature with grief ; and these perceive what the Spirit of truth speaketh in them.[2]

For he teacheth them to despise earthly, and to love heavenly things ; to neglect the world, and to desire heaven all the day and night.[3]

[1] Isa. xxix. [13].   [2] Ps. xxv. [5].   [3] Ps. i. [2].

CHAPTER V.

Of the Wonderful Effect of Divine Love.

I BLESS thee, O heavenly Father, Father of my Lord JESUS Christ, for that thou hast vouchsafed to remember me a poor creature.

O Father of mercies, and God of all comfort,[1] thanks be unto thee, who sometimes with thy comfort refreshest me, unworthy as I am of all comfort.

I will always bless and glorify thee, with thine only begotten Son, and the Holy Ghost, the Comforter, for ever and ever.

Ah, Lord God, thou holy lover of my soul, when thou comest into my heart, all that is within me shall rejoice.

Thou art my glory and the exultation of my heart : thou art my hope and refuge in the day of my tribulation.[2]

2. But because I am as yet weak in love, and imperfect in virtue, I have need to be strengthened and comforted by thee ; visit me therefore often, and instruct me with all holy discipline.

Set me free from evil passions, and heal my heart of all inordinate affections : that being inwardly cured and thoroughly cleansed, I may be made fit to love, courageous to suffer, steady to persevere.

3. Love is a great thing, yea, a great and thorough good ; by itself it makes everything that is heavy light, and it bears evenly all that is uneven.

For it carries a burden which is no burden,[3] and makes everything that is bitter, sweet and savoury.

[1] 2 Cor. i. [3].   [2] Ps. xxxii. [7], lix. [16].   [3] Matt. xi. [30].

The noble love of JESUS impels a man to do great things, and stirs him up to be always longing for what is more perfect.

Love desires to be on high, and will not be kept back by anything low and mean.

Love desires to be free, and estranged from all worldly affections, that so its inward sight may not be hindered ; that it may not be entangled by any temporal prosperity, or subdued by any adversity.

Nothing is sweeter than love, nothing more courageous, nothing higher, nothing wider, nothing more pleasant, nothing fuller nor better in heaven and earth ; because love is born of God, and cannot rest but in God, above all created things.

4. He that loveth, flieth, runneth, and rejoiceth ; he is free and is not bound.

He giveth all for all, and hath all in all ; because he resteth in One Highest above all things, from whom all that is good flows and proceeds.

He respecteth not the gifts, but turneth himself above all goods unto the giver.

Love oftentimes knoweth no bounds, but is fervent beyond all measure.

Love feels no burden, thinks nothing of trouble, attempts what is above its strength, pleads no excuse of impossibility ; for it thinks all things lawful for itself and all things possible.

It is therefore able to undertake all things, and it completes many things, and brings them to a conclusion, where he who does not love faints and lies down.

5. Love watcheth, and, sleeping, slumbereth not.[1]

---

[1] Rom. viii. [19].

Though weary, love is not tired ; though pressed, it is not straitened ; though alarmed, it is not confounded ; but as a lively flame and burning torch, it forces its way upwards, and securely passes through all.

If any man love, he knoweth what is the cry of this voice. For it is a loud cry in the ears of God, this ardent affection of the soul which saith, " My God, my Love, thou art all mine, and I am all thine."

6. Enlarge thou me in love, that, with the inward palate of my heart, I may taste how sweet it is to love, and to be dissolved, and as it were to bathe myself in thy love.

Let me be possessed by love, mounting above myself, through excessive fervour and admiration.

Let me sing the song of love, let me follow thee, my Beloved, on high ; let my soul spend itself in thy praise, rejoicing through love.

Let me love thee more than myself, and love myself only for thee ; and in thee all that truly love thee, as the law of love commandeth, shining out from thyself.

7. Love is active, sincere, affectionate, pleasant, and amiable ; courageous, patient, faithful, prudent, long-suffering, manly, and never seeking itself.[1]

For in whatever instance a person seeketh himself, there he falleth from love.[2]

Love is circumspect, humble, and upright ; not yielding to softness, or to levity, nor attending to vain things ; it is sober, chaste, steady, quiet, and guarded in all the senses.

---

[1] 1 Cor. xiii. [5].   [2] 1 Cor. x. [33] ; Phil. ii. [21].

Love is subject, and obedient to its superiors ; unto itself mean and despised, unto God devout and thankful, trusting and hoping always in him, even then when God imparteth no relish of sweetness unto it : for without sorrow none liveth in love.

8. He that is not prepared to suffer all things, and to stand to the will of his Beloved, is not worthy to be called a lover.

A lover ought to embrace willingly all that is hard and distasteful for the sake of his Beloved, and not to turn away from him on account of any contradictions.

CHAPTER VI.

Of the Proving of a True Lover.

MY son, thou art not yet a courageous and considerate lover.

WHEREFORE sayest thou this, O Lord ?

BECAUSE for a slight opposition thou givest over thy undertakings, and too eagerly seekest consolation.

A courageous lover standeth firm in temptations, and giveth no credit to the crafty persuasions of the enemy. As I please him in prosperity, so in adversity I am not unpleasing to him.[1]

2. A wise lover regardeth not so much the gift of him who loves him, as the love of the giver.

He esteems the good-will rather than the value

[1] Phil. iv. [11-13].

of the gift, and sets all gifts below him whom he loves.

A noble-minded lover resteth not in the gift, but in me above every gift.

All therefore is not lost, if sometimes thou thinkest less of me or my saints than thou wouldest.

That good and sweet affection which thou sometimes feelest, is the effect of grace present, and a sort of foretaste of thy heavenly home : but hereon thou must not lean too much, for it cometh and goeth.

But to strive against evil thoughts which may befall thee, and to reject [1] with scorn the suggestions of the devil, is a notable sign of virtue, and shall have great reward.

3. Let no strange fancies therefore trouble thee, which on any subject whatever may crowd into thy mind. Keep thy purpose with courage, and preserve an upright intention towards God.

Neither is it an illusion that sometimes thou art suddenly rapt on high, and presently returnest again unto the accustomed vanities of thy heart.

For these thou dost rather unwillingly suffer, than commit ; and so long as they displease thee, and thou strivest against them, it is matter of reward, and not of loss.

4. Know that the old enemy doth strive by all means to hinder thy desire to good, and to divert thee from all religious exercises ; particularly, from the reverent estimation of God's saints, from the devout commemoration of my passion, from the profitable remembrance of thy sins, from the guard

[1] Matt. iv. [10].

of thine own heart, and from the firm purpose of advancing in virtue.

Many evil thoughts does he suggest to thee, that so he may cause a wearisomeness and horror in thee, to call thee back from prayer and holy reading.

Humble confession is displeasing unto him ; and if he could, he would cause thee to cease from holy communion.

Trust him not, nor heed him, although he should often set snares of deceit to entrap thee.

Charge him with it, when he suggesteth evil and unclean thoughts unto thee ; say unto him,

" Away, thou unclean spirit ![1] blush, thou miserable wretch ! most unclean art thou that bringest such things into mine ears.

" Begone from me, thou wicked seducer ! thou shalt have no part in me : but JESUS shall be with me as a strong warrior, and thou shalt stand confounded.

" I had rather die, and undergo any torment, than consent unto thee.

" Hold thy peace and be silent ; I will hear thee no more, though thou shouldst work me many troubles. ' The Lord is my light and my salvation ; whom shall I fear ? ' [2]

" Though an host of men rose against me, yet should not my heart be afraid. The Lord is my helper and my Redeemer."

5. Fight like a good soldier : [3] and if thou sometimes fall through frailty, take again greater strength than before, trusting in my own abundant grace :

---

[1] Matt. iv. [10], xvi. [23].   [2] Ps. xxvii. [1].
[3] Ps. xxvii. [14] ; 1 Tim. vi. [12].

and take great heed of vain pleasing of thyself, and of pride.

Pride brings many into error, and makes them sometimes fall into blindness almost incurable.

Let the fall of the proud, thus foolishly presuming on their own strength, serve thee for a warning, and keep thee ever humble.

CHAPTER VII.

That Grace is to be Guarded by Humility.

MY son, it is more profitable for thee and more safe to conceal the grace of devotion ; not to lift thyself on high, nor to speak much thereof, nor to dwell much thereon ; but rather to despise thyself, and to fear lest the grace have been given to one unworthy of it.

This affection thou must not too earnestly cleave unto, for it may be quickly changed to the contrary.

Think when thou art in grace, how miserable and needy thou art wont to be without grace.

Nor is it in this only that thy progress in spiritual life consists, that thou hast the grace of comfort ; but rather that with humility, self-denial, and patience, thou endurest the withdrawing thereof ; provided thou do not then become listless in the exercise of prayer, nor suffer the rest of thy accustomed duties to be at all neglected.

Rather do thou cheerfully perform what lieth

in thee, according to the best of thy power and
understanding ; and do not wholly neglect thyself
because of the dryness or anxiety of mind which
thou feelest.

2. For there are many who, when things succeed
not well with them, presently become impatient
or slothful.

For the way of man is not always in his power,[1]
but it belongeth unto God to give, and to comfort,
when he will, and how much he will, and whom he
will ; as it shall please him, and no more.

Some unadvised persons, by reason of their
over-earnest desire of the grace of a devoted life,
have overthrown themselves ; because they at-
tempted more than they were able to perform,
not weighing the measure of their own weakness,
but following the desire of their heart rather than
the judgment of their reason.

And because they dwelt on greater matters than
was pleasing to God, they therefore quickly lost his
grace.

They who had built themselves nests [2] in heaven
were made helpless and vile outcasts ; to the end
that being humbled and impoverished, they might
learn not to fly with their own wings, but to trust
under my feathers.

They that are yet but novices and inexperienced
in the way of the Lord, unless they govern themselves by the counsel of discreet persons, may easily
be deceived and broken to pieces.

3. And if they will rather follow their own notions
than trust to others who are more experienced, their

[1] Jer. x. [23]; Rom. ix. [16].   [2] Isa. xiv. [13].

end will be dangerous, at least if they are unwilling to be drawn away from their own conceit.

It is seldom the case that they who are wise in their own conceit endure humbly to be governed by others.

Better it is to have a small portion of good sense, with humility [1] and a slender understanding, than great treasures of science with vain self-complacency.

Better it is for thee to have little, than much of that which may make thee proud.

He acts not very discreetly who wholly gives himself over to joy, forgetting his former helplessness, and that chastened fear of the Lord which is afraid of losing the grace which hath been offered.

Nor again is he very valiantly wise who, in time of adversity or any heaviness, at once yields too much to despairing thoughts, and reflects and thinks of me less trustfully than he ought.

4. He who in time of peace is willing to be over secure [2] shall be often found in time of war too much dejected and full of fears.

If thou couldest always continue humble and moderate within thyself, and also couldest thoroughly moderate and govern thy spirit, thou wouldest not so quickly fall into danger and offence.

It is good counsel, that when fervour of spirit is kindled within thee, thou shouldest consider how it will be when that light shall leave thee.

And when this happeneth, then remember that the light may return again, which, as a warning to thyself, and for mine own glory, I have withdrawn for a time. [3]

[1] Ps. xvi. [2], xvii. [10].   [2] 1 Thess. v. [6].   [3] Job. vii.

5. Such trials are oftentimes more profitable than if thou shouldst always have things prosper according to thy will.

For a man's worthiness is not to be estimated by the number of visions and comforts which he may have, or by his skill in the Scriptures, or by his being placed in high station.

But if he be grounded in true humility, and full of divine charity ; if he be always purely and sincerely seeking God's honour ; if he think nothing of and unfeignedly despise himself [1] and even rejoice more to be despised and made low by others, than to be honoured by them.

CHAPTER VIII.

Of a Mean Conceit of Ourselves in the Sight of God.

SHALL I speak unto my Lord, who am but dust and ashes ? [2] If I esteem myself to be anything more, behold, thou standest against me, and my inquities bear true witness, and I cannot contradict it.

But if I abase myself, and reduce myself to nothing, and shrink from all self-esteem, and grind myself to the dust I am, thy grace will be favourable to me, and thy light near unto my heart ; and all self-esteem, how little soever, shall be swallowed up in the valley of my nothingness, and perish for ever.

There thou showest thyself unto me, what I am,

[1] Ps. lxxxiv. [10].   [2] Gen. xviii. [27].

what I have been, and whither I am come ; for I am nothing, and I knew it not.

If I be left to myself, behold, I become nothing but mere weakness ; but if thou for an instant look upon me, I am forthwith made strong, and am filled with new joy.

And a great marvel it is, that I am so suddenly lifted up, and so graciously embraced by thee, who of mine own weight am always sinking downward.

2. Thy love is the cause hereof, freely preventing me, and relieving me in so many necessities, guarding me also from pressing dangers, and snatching me (as I may truly say) from evils out of number.

For indeed by loving myself amiss, I lost myself ;[1] and by seeking thee alone, and purely loving thee, I have found both myself and thee, and by that love have more deeply reduced myself to nothing.

Because thou, O dearest Lord, dealest with me above all desert, and above all that I dare hope or ask.

3. Blessed be thou, my God : for although I be unworthy of any benefits, yet thy royal bounty and infinite goodness never cease to do good even to the ungrateful,[2] and to those who are turned away far from thee.

Turn thou us unto thee, that we may be thankful, humble, and devout ; for thou art our salvation, our courage, and our strength.

[1] John xii. [25].   [2] Matt. v. [45].

CHAPTER IX.

*That all Things are to be Referred unto God, as
their Last End.*

MY son, I ought to be thy supreme and ultimate
end, if thou desire to be truly blessed.

By this intention thy affections will be purified,
which are too often inordinately inclined to selfishness and unto creatures.

For if in anything thou seekest thyself, immediately thou faintest and driest up.

I would therefore thou shouldst refer all things
principally unto me, for I am he who have given all.

Consider everything as flowing from the Highest
Good ; [1] and therefore unto me as their original all
must be brought back.

2. From me, as from a living fountain, the small
and the great, the poor and the rich, do draw the
water of life ; [2] and they that willingly and freely
serve me shall receive grace for grace.

But he who desires to glory in things out of me, [3]
or to take pleasure in some private good, shall
not be grounded in true joy, nor be enlarged in his
heart, but shall many ways be encumbered and
straitened.

Thou oughtest therefore to ascribe nothing of
good to thyself, nor do thou attribute goodness unto
any man ; but give all unto God, without whom man
hath nothing.

I have given thee all, [4] and my will is to have thee

[1] Ecclus. i. [5].   [2] John iv. [14].
[3] 1 Cor. i. [29].   [4] 1 Cor. iv. [6].

all again ; and with great strictness do I exact from thee a return of thanks.

3. This is the truth whereby vainglory is put to flight.

And if heavenly grace enter in and true charity, there will be no envy nor narrowness of heart, neither will self-love busy itself.

For divine charity overcometh all things, and enlargeth all the powers of the soul.

If thou rightly judge, thou wilt rejoice in me alone, in me alone thou wilt hope ; for none is good save God alone,[1] who is to be praised above all things, and in all to be blessed.

CHAPTER X.

That to Despise the World and Serve God is Sweet.

Now I will speak again, O Lord, and will not be silent ; I will say in the ears of my God, my Lord, and my King, who is on high : " O how great is the abundance of thy goodness, O Lord, which thou hast laid up for them that fear thee." [2]

But what art thou to those who love thee ? what to those who serve thee with their whole heart ?

Truly unspeakable is the sweetness of contemplating thee, which thou bestowest on them that love thee.

In this especially thou hast showed me the sweetness of thy love : that when I was not, thou madest

---

[1] Matt. xix. [17] ; Luke xviii. [12].　　[2] Ps. xxxi. [19].

me ; when I went far astray from thee, thou broughtest me back again, that I might serve thee ; and that thou hast commanded me to love thee.[1]

2. O Fountain of love unceasing, what shall I say concerning thee ?

How can I forget thee, who hast vouchsafed to remember me, even after I had wasted away and perished ?

Thou hast showed mercy to thy servant beyond all expectation, and hast exhibited favour and loving-kindness beyond all desert.

What return shall I make to thee for this grace ?[2] For it is not granted to all to forsake all, to renounce the world, and to undertake a life of religious retirement.

Is it any great thing that I should serve thee,[3] whom the whole creation is bound to serve ?

It ought not to seem much to me, to serve thee ; but rather this doth appear much to me, and wonderful, that thou vouchsafest to receive into thy service one so poor and unworthy, and to make him one with thy beloved servants.

3. Behold, all things are thine which I have, and whereby I serve thee ?[4]

And yet contrariwise, thou rather servest me than I thee.

Behold, heaven and earth, which thou hast created for the service of man, are ready at hand, and do daily perform whatever thou hast commanded.

And this is little : thou hast moreover also appointed angels to minister to man.[5]

[1] Gen. i. [27]; Ps. cxix. [73]; Matt. xv. [2] Ps. cxvi. [1].
[3] Judges xvi. [15]. [4] 1 Cor. iv. [7]. [5] Ps. xci. [11]; Heb. i. [14].

But that which excelleth all is this, that thou thyself hast vouchsafed to serve man, and hast promised that thou wouldst give thyself unto him.

4. What shall I give thee for all these thousands of benefits ? I would I could serve thee all the days of my life.

I would I were able, at least for one day, to do thee some worthy service.

Truly thou art worthy of all service, of all honour, and everlasting praise.

Truly thou art my Lord, and I thy poor servant, who am bound to serve thee with all my might, neither ought I ever to be weary of praising thee.

And this I wish to do, this I desire : and whatsoever is wanting unto me, do thou, I beseech thee, vouchsafe to supply.

5. It is a great honour, and a great glory, to serve thee, and to despise all things for thee.

For great grace shall be given to those who shall have willingly subjected themselves to thy most holy service.

They who for thy love shall have renounced all carnal delights, shall find the sweetest consolations of the Holy Ghost.[1]

They shall attain great freedom of mind who for thy name's sake enter into the narrow way,[2] and have left off all worldly care.

6. O sweet and delightful service of God,[3] by which a man is made truly free and holy !

O sacred state of religious service, which makes a man equal to the angels, pleasing to God, terrible

---

[1] Matt. xix. [29].   [2] Matt. vii. [14].
[3] Matt. xi. [30] ; 1 John v. [3].

to devils, and worthy to be commended of all the faithful !

O welcome service and ever to be desired, in which we are rewarded with the Greatest Good, and attain to joy which shall endlessly remain with us !

CHAPTER XI.

That the Longings and Desires of our Hearts are to be Examined and Moderated.

MY son, thou must still learn many things which thou hast not yet well learned.

WHAT are these, O Lord ?

THAT thou frame thy desires [1] wholly according to my good pleasure ; and that thou be not a lover of thyself, but an earnest follower of my will.

Various longings and desires oftentimes inflame thee, and drive thee forwards with vehemence : but do thou consider whether thou be not moved rather for thine own advantage, than for my honour.

If I be the cause, thou wilt be well content howsoever I shall ordain ; but if there lurk in thee any self-seeking, [2] behold, this it is that hindereth thee and weigheth thee down.

2. Beware, therefore, thou lean not too much upon any desire, conceived without asking my counsel, lest perhaps afterwards it repent thee, or thou be displeased with that which at first pleased thee, and which thou desiredst earnestly, as the best.

[1] Ps. cviii. [1] ; Matt. vi. [10].   [2] Phil. ii. [21].

For not every affection which seems good is immediately to be followed ; nor, on the other hand, is every contrary affection at the first to be avoided.

It is sometimes expedient to use a restraint even in good desires and endeavours, lest through unseasonable effort thou incur distraction of mind ; lest by thy want of self-government thou beget a scandal unto others ; or again, being by others thwarted and resisted, thou become suddenly confounded, and so fall.

3. Sometimes, however, thou must use violence,[1] and resist manfully thine appetite, not regarding what the flesh would or would not ;[2] but rather taking pains that even perforce it may be made subject to the Spirit.[3]

And so long ought it to be chastened and to be forced to remain under servitude, until it be prepared for everything, and learn to be content with a little, and to be pleased with plain and simple things, and not to murmur against any inconvenience.

CHAPTER XII.

Of the Growth of Patience in the Soul, and of Striving against Concupiscence.

O LORD my God, patience is very necessary for me,[4] for I perceive that many things in this life do fall out as we would not.

---

[1] Phil. ii. [11].   [2] Rom. viii. [1–13] ; 2 Cor. iv. [10], x. [3].
[3] 1 Cor. ix. [27].   [4] Heb. x. [36].

For whatsoever plans I shall devise for my own peace, my life cannot be without war and affliction.[1]

It is so, my son. But my will is, that thou seek not that peace which is void of temptations, or which suffereth nothing contrary; but rather think that thou hast found peace, when thou art exercised with sundry tribulations,[2] and tried in many adversities.

2. If thou say that thou art not able to suffer much, how then wilt thou endure the fire hereafter?

Of two evils the less is alway to be chosen. That thou mayest therefore avoid the everlasting punishment that is to come, endeavour to endure present evils patiently for God's sake.

Dost thou think that the men of this world suffer nothing or but a little? Ask even of those who live most at ease, and thou shalt find it otherwise.

But thou wilt say, they have many delights, and follow their own wills, and therefore they do not much weigh their own afflictions.

Be it so, that they have whatsoever they will; but how long dost thou think that it will last?

3. Behold, the wealthy of this world shall consume away like smoke,[3] and there shall be no memory of their past joys!

Yea, even while they are yet alive, they do not rest in them without bitterness, and weariness, and fear.

For from the self-same thing in which they delight they oftentimes receive the penalty of sorrow.

And it is but just that having inordinately sought

---

[1] Job vii. [1].   [2] James i. [2].   [3] Ps. lxviii. [2].

and followed after pleasures, they should enjoy them not without shame and bitterness.

4. Oh how brief, how false, how inordinate and base, are all those pleasures !

Yet so drunken and blind are men, that they understand it not ; but like dumb beasts, for the poor enjoyment of a corruptible life, they incur the death of the soul.

Thou therefore, my son, " go not after thy lusts, but refrain thyself from thine appetites." [1] " Delight thyself in the LORD, and he shall give thee the desires of thine heart." [2]

5. For if thou desire true delight, and to be more plentifully comforted by me, behold, in the contempt of all worldly things, and in the cutting off all base delights, shall be thy blessing, and abundant comfort shall be given thee.

And the more thou withdraw thyself from all solace of creatures, so much the sweeter and more powerful consolations shalt thou find in me.

But at the first thou shalt not without some sadness, nor without a laborious conflict, attain unto them.

Old inbred habit will, for a time, resist, but by a better way it shall be entirely overcome.

The flesh will murmur against thee ; but with fervency of spirit thou shalt bridle it.

The old serpent will tempt and trouble thee, but by prayer he shall be put to flight. Moreover also, by useful work thou shalt greatly stop the way against him.

[1] Ecclus. xviii. [30].   [2] Ps. xxxvii. [4].

CHAPTER XIII.

Of Humble Obedience after the Example of Jesus Christ.

My son, he that endeavoureth to withdraw himself from obedience, withdraweth himself from grace; and he who seeketh for himself private benefits,[1] loseth those which are common.

He that doth not cheerfully and freely submit himself to his superior, showeth that his flesh is not as yet perfectly brought into subjection, but oftentimes struggleth and murmureth against him.

Learn thou therefore quickly to submit thyself to thy superior, if thou desire to keep thine own flesh under the yoke.

For more speedily is the outward enemy overcome, if the inward man be not in disorder.

There is no worse enemy, nor one more troublesome to the soul, than thou art unto thyself, if thou be not in harmony with the Spirit.

It is altogether necessary that thou conceive a true contempt for thyself, if thou desire to prevail against flesh and blood.

2. Because thou still lovest thyself inordinately, thou art afraid to resign thyself wholly to the will of others.

And yet, what great matter is it,[2] if thou, who art but dust and nothing, subject thyself to a man for God's sake, when I, the Almighty and the Most Highest, who created all things of nothing, humbly subjected myself to man for thy sake?

[1] Matt. xvi. [24].   [2] Luke ii. [7]; John xiii. [14].

I became of all men the most humble and the most abject, that thou mightest overcome thy pride with my humility.

O dust, learn to be obedient. Learn to humble thyself, thou earth and clay, and to bow thyself down under the feet of all men.

Learn to break thine own will, and to yield thyself to all subjection.

3. Be zealous against thyself, and suffer no pride to dwell in thee; but show thyself so humble and so lowly, that all may be able to walk over thee, and to tread thee down as the mire of the streets. Vain man, what hast thou to complain of?

What canst thou answer, vile sinner, to them that upbraid thee, thou who hast so often offended God, and hast so many times deserved hell?

But mine eye spared thee, because thy soul was precious in my sight; that thou mightest know my love, and ever be thankful for my benefits;

Also that thou mightest continually give thyself to true subjection and humility, and endure patiently to be despised.

CHAPTER XIV.

Of Considering the Secret Judgments of God that so we be not lifted up for anything good in us.

THOU, O Lord, thunderest forth thy judgments over me, thou shakest all my bones with fear and trembling, and my soul is very sore afraid.

I stand astonished; and I consider "that the heavens are not pure in thy sight." [1]

If in angels thou didst find wickedness,[2] and didst not spare even them, what shall become of me?

Even stars fell from heaven;[3] what then can I presume who am but dust?

They whose works seemed commendable, have fallen into the lowest misery; and those who did eat the bread of angels,[4] I have seen delighting themselves with the husks of swine.

2. There is therefore no holiness, if thou, O Lord, withdraw thine hand.

No wisdom availeth, if thou cease to guide.

No courage helpeth, if thou leave off to defend.

No chastity is secure, if thou do not protect it.

No vigilance of our own availeth, if thy sacred watchfulness be not present with us.

For, if we be left of thee, we sink and perish; but being visited of thee, we are raised up and live.

Truly we are inconstant, but by thee we are established; we wax lukewarm, but by thee we are inflamed.

3. Oh how humbly and meanly ought I to think of myself! how ought I to esteem it as nothing, if I seem to have any good in me!

With what profound humility ought I to submit myself to thine unfathomable judgments, O Lord; where I find myself to be nothing else than nothing, and very nothing!

O weight that cannot be measured! O sea that

---

[1] Job xv. [15]. [2] Job iv. [18].
[3] Rev. viii. [10]. [4] Ps. lxxviii. [25].

cannot be passed over, where I discover nothing of myself save only and wholly nothing !

Where then can glorying hide itself ? where can be trust in mine own virtue ?

All vainglorying is swallowed up in the deep of thy judgments over me.

4. What is all flesh in thy sight ?

Shall the clay boast against Him that formed it ?

How can he be lifted up with vain words, whose heart is truly subject to God ? [1]

Not all the world will make him proud whom the truth hath subjected unto itself ; neither shall he who hath firmly settled his whole hope in God be moved by the tongues of all his flatterers.

For even they themselves who speak, behold they all are nothing, for they will pass away with the sound of their words : but the truth of the Lord remaineth for ever.[2]

CHAPTER XV.

*In everything which we Desire, how we ought to Feel,
and what we ought to Say.*

MY son, say thou thus in everything : " Lord, if this be pleasing unto thee, so let it be.[3]

" Lord, if it be to thy honour, in thy name let this be done.

" Lord, if thou see it to be expedient, and know it

---

[1] Isa. xxix. [16] ; Ecclus. xxiii. [4, 5].
[2] Ps. cxvii. [2].   [3] James iii.

to be profitable for me, then grant unto me that I may use this to thine honour.

" But if thou know it will be hurtful unto me, and no profit to the health of my soul, take away the desire from me."

For not every desire proceedeth from the Holy Spirit, even though it seem unto a man right and good.

It is difficult to judge truly whether a good spirit or the contrary be urging thee to desire this or that ; or whether by thine own spirit thou be moved thereunto.

Many have been deceived in the end who at the first seemed to be led by a good spirit.

2. Therefore whatsoever seemeth to be desirable, must always be desired and prayed for in the fear of God and with humility of heart ; and chiefly thou must commit the whole matter to me with special resignation of thyself, and thou must say,—

" O Lord, thou knowest what is best for us, let this or that be done, as thou pleasest.

" Give what thou wilt, and how much thou wilt, and when thou wilt.

" Deal with me as thou thinkest good, and as best pleaseth thee, and is most for thy honour.

" Set me where thou wilt, and deal with me in all things just as thou wilt.

" I am in thy hand ; turn me round, and turn me back again, as thou shalt please.

" Behold, I am thy servant, prepared for all things ; for I desire not to live unto myself, but unto thee ; and oh that I could do it worthily and perfectly ! "

A Prayer that the will of God may be fulfilled.

3. O MOST merciful JESUS, grant to me thy grace, that it may be with me, and work with me,[1] and continue with me even to the end.

Grant that I may always desire and will that which is to thee most acceptable and most dear.

Let thy will be mine, and let my will ever follow thine, and agree perfectly with it.

Let my will be all one with thine, and let me not be able to will, or anything to forego, but what thou willest or dost not will.

4. Grant that I may die to all things that are in the world, and for thy sake may love to be contemned, and not to be known in this generation.

Grant to me above all things that I can desire, to desire to rest in thee, and in thee to have my heart at peace.

Thou art the true peace of the heart : thou art its only rest ; out of thee all things are full of trouble and unrest. In this peace, that is, in thee, the one chiefest eternal Good, I will lay me down and sleep.[2]   *Amen.*

CHAPTER XVI.

That True Comfort is to be Sought in God alone.

WHATSOEVER I can desire or imagine for my comfort, I look for it not here but hereafter.

For if I alone should possess all the comforts

---

[1] Wisd. ix. [10].   [2] Ps. iv. [8].

of the world, and might enjoy all the delights thereof,[1] it is certain that they could not long endure.

Wherefore, O my soul, thou canst not be fully comforted,[2] nor have perfect refreshment, except in God, the comforter of the poor, and the helper of the humble.

Wait a little while, O my soul, wait for the divine promise, and thou shalt have abundance of all good things in heaven.

If thou desire beyond measure the things that are present, thou shalt lose those which are heavenly and eternal.

Use temporal things, and desire eternal.

Thou canst not be satisfied by any temporal goods, because thou art not created to enjoy them.

2. Although thou shouldst possess all created good, yet couldst thou not be happy thereby nor blessed ; but in God, who created all things, consisteth thy whole blessedness and felicity.[3]

Not such happiness as is seen and commended by the foolish lovers of the world, but such as the good and faithful servants of Christ wait for, and of which the spiritual and pure in heart, whose conversation is in heaven,[4] sometimes have a foretaste.

Vain and brief is all human consolation.

Blessed and true is the consolation which is received inwardly from the truth.

A devout man beareth everywhere about with him his own comforter JESUS, and saith unto him, " Be

---

[1] Matt. xvi. [26]. [2] Ps. lxxvii. [1, 2].
[3] Wisd. ii. [23]. [4] Phil. iii. [20].

thou present with me, O Lord JESU, in every time and place.

"Let this be my comfort, to be willing to lack all human comfort.

"And if thy comfort be wanting, let thy will and just proving of me be unto me as the greatest comfort ; for thou wilt not always be angry, neither wilt thou chide for ever."[1]

CHAPTER XVII.

That all our Anxieties are to be Rested on God.

MY son, suffer me to do with thee what I please. I know what is expedient for thee.

Thou thinkest as man ; thou judgest in many things as human affection persuadeth thee.

O LORD, what thou sayest is true. Thy care for me is greater [2] than all the care that I can take for myself.

For he standeth but very unsafely who casteth not all his care upon thee.

O Lord, if only my will may remain right and firm towards thee, do with me whatsoever it shall please thee.

For it cannot be anything but good, whatsoever thou shalt do with me.

2. If it be thy will that I should be in darkness, be thou blessed ; and if it be thy will that I should be

---

[1] Ps. ciii. [9].   [2] Matt. vi. [30] ; John vi.

in light, be thou again blessed. If thou vouchsafe to comfort me, be thou blessed ; and if thou wilt have me afflicted, be thou blessed also.

MY son, such as this ought to be thy state, if thou desire to walk with me.

Thou oughtest to be as ready to suffer as to rejoice.

Thou oughtest as cheerfully to be destitute and poor as to be full and rich.

3. O LORD, for thy sake I will cheerfully suffer [1] whatsoever shall come upon me with thy permission.

From thy hand I am willing to receive indifferently good and evil, sweet and bitter, joy and sorrow ; and for all that befalleth me I will be thankful.

Keep me safe from all sin, and I shall fear neither death [2] nor hell.

So thou do not cast me from thee for ever, nor blot me out of the book of life, what tribulation soever befalleth me shall not hurt me.

CHAPTER XVIII.

That Temporal Sufferings must be borne Patiently, after the Example of Christ.

MY son, I descended from heaven [3] for thy salvation ; I took upon me thy sorrows,[4] not necessity but love drawing me thereto ; that thou thyself

---

[1] Job ii. [10].   [2] Ps. xxiii. [4].
[3] John iii. [13].   [4] Isa. liii. [4].

mightest learn patience, and bear temporal sufferings without repining.

For from the hour of my birth,[1] even until my death on the cross, I was not without suffering of grief.

I suffered great want of things temporal ; I often heard many murmurings against me ; I endured patiently disgraces and revilings ; in return for benefits I received ingratitude ; for miracles, blasphemies ; for heavenly doctrine, reproofs.

2. O LORD, for that thou wert patient in thy lifetime, herein especially fulfilling the commandment of thy Father ; [2] it is reason that I, a most miserable sinner, should bear myself patiently according to thy will, and for my soul's welfare endure the burden of this corruptible life as long as thou thyself shalt choose.

For although this present life be burdensome, yet notwithstanding it is now by thy grace made very gainful ; and by thine example and the footsteps of thy saints, more bright and clear, and endurable to the weak.

It is also much more full of consolation than it was formerly under the old law, when the gate of heaven remained shut ; and the way also to heaven seemed more dark, when so few cared to seek after the kingdom of heaven.[3]

Moreover also, they who then were just and such as should be saved, could not enter into the heavenly kingdom before the accomplishment of thy passion, and the payment of the debt of thy holy death.

[1] Luke ii. [7].   [2] John v. [30].   [3] Matt. vii. [14].

3. O how great thanks am I bound to render unto thee, that thou hast vouchsafed to show unto me and to all faithful people the good and the right way to thine eternal kingdom.

For thy life is our way, and by the path of holy patience we walk toward thee, who art our Crown.

If thou hadst not gone before us and taught us, who would have cared to follow!

Alas, how many would remain behind and afar off, if they considered not thy glorious example!

Behold, we are even yet lukewarm, though we have heard of so many of thy miracles and doctrines. What would become of us if we had not so great light [1] whereby to follow thee?

CHAPTER XIX.

Of the Endurance of Injuries, and of the Proof of True Patience.

WHAT is it thou sayest, my son? Cease to complain, when thou considerest my passion, and the sufferings of my other saints.

Thou hast not yet resisted unto blood. [2]

It is but little which thou sufferest, in comparison of those who suffered so much, who were so strongly tempted, so grievously afflicted, so many ways tried and exercised. [3]

Thou oughtest therefore to call to mind the more

[1] John xii. [46].　　[2] Heb. xii. [4].　　[3] Heb. xi. [37].

heavy sufferings of others, that so thou mayest the more easily bear thine own very small troubles.

And if they seem unto thee not very small, then beware lest thine impatience be the cause thereof.

However, whether they be small or whether they be great, endeavour patiently to undergo them all.

2. The better thou disposest thyself to suffering, the more wisely thou doest, and the greater reward shalt thou receive. Thou shalt also more easily endure it, if both in mind and by habit thou art diligently prepared thereunto.

Do not say, " I cannot endure to suffer these things at the hands of such an one, nor ought I to endure things of this sort ; for he hath done me great wrong, and reproacheth me with things which I never thought of ; but of another I will willingly suffer—that is, if they are things which I shall see I ought to suffer."

Such a thought is foolish : it considereth not the virtue of patience, nor by whom it will be to be crowned ; but rather, weigheth too exactly the persons, and the injuries offered to itself.

3. He is not truly patient who is willing to suffer only so much as he thinks good, and from whom he pleases.

But the truly patient man minds not by whom he is exercised, whether by his superiors, by one of his equals, or by an inferior ; whether by a good and holy man, or by one that is perverse and unworthy.

But indifferently from every creature, how much soever, or how often soever anything adverse befall him, he takes it all thankfully as from the hands of God, and esteems it great gain :

For with God it is impossible that anything, how small soever, if only it be suffered for God's sake, should pass without its reward.

4. Be thou therefore prepared for the fight, if thou wilt win the victory.

Without a combat thou canst not attain unto the crown of patience.[1]

If thou art unwilling to suffer, thou refusest to be crowned. But if thou desire to be crowned, fight manfully, endure patiently.

Without labour there is no rest, nor without fighting can the victory be won.

O Lord, let that become possible to me by thy grace which by nature seems impossible to me.

Thou knowest that I am able to suffer but little, and that I am quickly cast down when a slight adversity ariseth.

For thy name's sake, let every exercise of tribulation be made pleasant unto me; for to suffer and to be troubled for thy sake is very wholesome for my soul.

CHAPTER XX.

Of the Acknowledging of our own Infirmities, and of the Sufferings of this Life.

I WILL acknowledge my sin unto thee;[2] I will confess mine infirmity unto thee, O Lord.

[1] 2 Tim. ii. [3-5].　　　[2] Ps. xxxii. [5].

Oftentimes a small matter it is that makes me sad and dejected.

I resolve to act with courage, but when even a small temptation comes, I am at once in a great strait.

It is sometimes a very trifle whence a great temptation arises.

And whilst I think myself safe, and when I least expect it, I sometimes find myself overcome by all but a slight breath.

2. Behold therefore, O Lord, my low estate,[1] and my frailty, which is in every way known unto thee.

Have mercy on me, and deliver me out of the mire, that I may not stick fast therein,[2] and may not remain utterly cast down for ever.

This is that which oftentimes strikes me down, and confounds me in thy sight, that I am so subject to fall, and so weak in resisting my passions.

And although I do not altogether consent, yet their continued assaults are troublesome and grievous unto me; and it is very exceedingly irksome to live thus daily in conflict.

Hereby doth my weakness become known unto me, in that hateful fancies do always much more easily invade than forsake me.

3. Most mighty God of Israel, thou zealous lover of faithful souls! O that thou wouldst consider the labour and sorrow of thy servant, and assist him in all things whatsoever he undertaketh.

Strengthen me with heavenly courage, lest the old man, the miserable flesh, not as yet fully subject to the Spirit, prevail and get the upper hand.

[1] Ps. xxv. [18].   [2] Ps. lxix. [14].

Against this it will be needful for me to fight as long as I breathe in this miserable life.

Alas, what a life is this, where tribulation and miseries are never wanting ; where all is full of snares and enemies !

For when one tribulation or temptation goeth, another cometh ; yea, and while the first conflict is yet lasting, many others come unexpected one after another.

4. And how can a life be loved that hath so many imbitterments, and is subject to so many calamities and miseries ?

How, too, can it be called a life that begetteth so many deaths and plagues ?

And yet it is the object of men's love, and its delights are sought of many.

The world is oftentimes blamed for being deceitful and vain, and yet men do not easily part with it because the desires of the flesh bear so great a sway.

But some things draw us to love the world, others to contemn it.

The lust of the flesh, the lust of the eyes, and the pride of life,[1] do draw us to the love of the world ; but the pains and miseries that justly follow them cause a hatred of the world and a loathing thereof.

5. But, alas ! the fondness for vicious pleasures overcometh the mind of him who is given to the world ; and he esteemeth it a delight to be ever under thorns,[2] because he hath neither seen nor tasted the sweetness of God and the inward pleasantness of virtue.

[1] 1 John ii. [16].   [2] Job xxx. [7].

But they who perfectly contemn the world, and study to live to God under holy discipline, these are not ignorant of the divine sweetness promised to those who truly forsake the world. They also very clearly see how grievously the world erreth, and how it is in many ways deceived.

CHAPTER XXI.

That we are to Rest in God above all his Gifts and Benefits.

ABOVE all things, and in all things, O my soul, thou shalt rest in the Lord alway, for he himself is the everlasting rest of the saints.

Grant me, O most sweet and loving JESUS, to rest in thee, above all creatures,[1] above all health and beauty, above all glory and honour, above all power and dignity, above all knowledge and subtilty, above all riches and arts, above all joy and gladness, above all fame and praise, above all sweetness and comfort, above all hope and promise, above all desert and desire :

Above all gifts and benefits that thou canst give and impart unto us, above all mirth and joy that the mind of man can receive and feel :

Finally, above angels and archangels, and above all the heavenly host, above all things visible and invisible, and above all that thou art not, O my God.

[1] Rom. viii. [19–22].

2. Because thou, O Lord my God, art supremely good above all; thou alone art most high, thou alone most powerful, thou alone most full and sufficient, thou alone most sweet and most full of consolation.

Thou alone art most lovely and loving, thou alone most noble and glorious above all things, in whom all good things together both perfectly are, and ever have been, and shall be.

And therefore whatsoever thou bestowest on me besides thyself, or revealest unto me of thyself, or promisest, is but mean and unsatisfying, whilst thou art not seen and not fully obtained.

For surely my heart cannot truly rest, nor be entirely contented, unless it rest in thee, and rise above all gifts and all creatures whatsoever.

3. O thou most beloved spouse of my soul, JESU Christ, thou most pure Lover, thou Lord of all creation; O that I had the wings of true liberty, that I might flee away and rest in thee! [1]

O when shall it be fully granted me to consider in quietness of mind, and to see how sweet thou art, my Lord God!

When shall I fully gather up myself unto thee, that by reason of my love to thee I may not feel myself, but thee alone, above all sense and measure, in a manner not known unto every one! [2]

But now I oftentimes sigh, and bear my unhappiness with grief:

Because many evils occur in this vale of miseries which do often trouble, grieve, and over-cloud me; often hinder and distract me, allure and entangle

[1] Ps. lv. [6].   [2] Dan. x.

me, so that I can have no free access unto thee, nor enjoy the sweet welcomings which are ever ready for the blessed spirits.

O let my sighs move thee and my manifold desolation here on earth.

4. O JESU, thou brightness of eternal glory, thou comfort of the pilgrim soul, with thee is my tongue without voice, and my very silence speaketh unto thee.

How long doth my Lord delay to come?

Let him come unto me his poor despised servant, and let him make me glad. Let him put forth his hand, and deliver his poor servant from all anguish.

Come, O come; for without thee I shall have no joyful day nor hour; for thou art my joy, and without thee my table is empty.

A wretched creature am I, and as it were imprisoned and loaded with fetters, until thou refresh me with the light of thy presence, and grant me liberty, and show a friendly countenance toward me.

5. Let others seek what they please instead of thee; but for me, nothing else doth nor shall delight me, but thou only, my God, my hope, my everlasting salvation.

I will not hold my peace, nor cease to pray until thy grace return again, and thou speak inwardly unto me.

BEHOLD, here I am. Behold, I come unto thee, because thou hast called upon me. Thy tears and the desire of thy soul, thy humiliation and thy contrition of heart, have inclined and brought me unto thee.

And I said, LORD, I have called thee, and have desired to enjoy thee, being ready to refuse all things for thy sake.

For thou first hast stirred me up that I might seek thee.

Blessed be thou therefore, O Lord, that hast showed this goodness to thy servant, according to the multitude of thy mercies.

6. What hath thy servant more to say before thee ? he can only greatly humble himself in thy sight, ever mindful of his own iniquity and vileness.

For there is none like unto thee [1] in all whatsoever is wonderful in heaven and earth.

Thy works are very good, thy judgments true, and by thy providence the universe is governed.

Praise therefore and glory be unto thee, O wisdom of the Father : let my mouth, my soul, and all creatures together, praise and bless thee.

CHAPTER XXII.

Of the Remembrance of God's manifold Benefits.

OPEN, O Lord, my heart in thy law, and teach me to walk in thy commandments.[2]

Grant me to understand thy will, and with great reverence and diligent consideration to remember thy benefits, as well in general as in particular, that henceforward I may be able worthily to give thee thanks.

---

[1] Ps. lxxxvi. [8].   [2] Ps. cxix.

But I know and confess that I am not able, even in the least matter, to give thee due thanks for the favours which thou bestowest upon me.

I am less than the least of all thy benefits : and when I consider thy noble bounty, the greatness thereof maketh my spirit to faint.

2. All that we have in our soul and body, and whatsoever we possess outwardly or inwardly, naturally or supernaturally, are thy benefits, and do speak thee bountiful, merciful, and good, from whom we have received all good things.

Although one have received more, another less, all notwithstanding are thine, and without thee even the least blessing cannot be had.

He that hath received the greatest cannot glory of his own desert, nor extol himself above others, nor insult over the lesser. For he is the greatest and the best who ascribeth least unto himself, and who in rendering thanks is the most humble and most devout.

And he that esteemeth himself viler than all men, and judgeth himself most unworthy, is fittest to receive greater blessings.

3. But he that hath received fewer ought not to be out of heart, nor to take it grievously, nor to envy them that are enriched with greater store, but rather to turn his mind to thee, and highly to praise thy goodness, for that thou bestowest thy gifts so bountifully, so freely, and so willingly, without respect of persons.

All things proceed from thee, and therefore in all things thou art to be praised.

Thou knowest what is fit to be given to every

one. And why this man hath less and that man more, it is not for us to judge, but for thee who dost exactly know what is meet for every one.

4. Wherefore, O Lord God, I even esteem it a great mercy not to have much of that which outwardly and in the opinion of men seems worthy of glory and applause.

He who considereth the poverty and unworthiness of his own person, should be so far from conceiving grief or sadness, or from being cast down thereat, that he rather should take great comfort and be glad.

For thou, O God, hast chosen the poor and humble and the despised of this world for thyself,[1] to be thy familiar friends and servants.

Witnesses are thine apostles themselves, whom thou hast made princes over all the earth.[2]

And yet they lived in the world without complaint,[3] so humble and simple, without all malice and deceit, that they even rejoiced to suffer reproach for thy name;[4] and what the world abhorreth they embraced with great affection.

5. When therefore a man loveth thee and acknowledgeth thy benefits, nothing ought so to rejoice him as thy will toward him, and the good pleasure of thine eternal appointment.

And herewith he ought to be so contented and comforted, that he would as willingly be the least as another would wish to be the greatest.

He would, too, be as peaceable and contented in the last place as in the first; as willing to be

[1] 1 Cor. i. [27, 28].   [2] Ps. xlv. [16].
[3] 1 Thess. ii. [10].   [4] Acts v. [41].

spised castaway, of no name or character, as
    e preferred in honour before others, and to be
greater in the world than they.

For thy will and the love of thy glory ought
to be preferred before all things, and to comfort
him more, and to please him better, than all the
benefits which either he hath received or may
receive.

CHAPTER XXIII.

Of Four Things that bring great Inward Peace.

MY son, now will I teach thee the way of peace
and of true liberty.

O LORD, I beseech thee, do as thou sayest, for
this is delightful to me to hear.

BE desirous, my son, to do the will of another
rather than thine own.[1]

Choose always to have less rather than more.[2]

Seek always the lowest place, and to be beneath
every one.[3]

Wish always, and pray, that the will of God may
be wholly fulfilled in thee.[4]

Behold, such a man entereth within the borders
of peace and rest.

2. O LORD, this short discourse of thine con-
taineth within itself much perfection.[5]

[1] Matt. xxvi. [39]; John v. [30], vi. [38].   [2] 1 Cor. x. [24].
[3] Luke xiv. [10].   [4] Matt. vi. [10].   [5] Matt. v. [48].

It is little in words, but full of meaning, and abundant in fruit.

For if it could faithfully be kept by me, I should not be so easily disturbed.

For as often as I feel myself unquiet and weighed down, I find that I have strayed from this doctrine.

But thou who canst do all things, and ever lovest the profiting of my soul, increase in me thy grace, that I may be able to fulfil thy words, and to work out mine own salvation.

A Prayer against evil thoughts.

3. O LORD my God, be not thou far from me; my God, haste thee to help me ;[1] for there have risen up against me sundry thoughts and great fears afflicting my soul.

How shall I pass through unhurt ? how shall I break them to pieces ?

" I (saith he) will go before thee, and will humble the great ones of the earth ; I will open the doors of the prison, and reveal unto thee hidden secrets." [2]

Do, O Lord, as thou sayest, and let all evil thoughts fly from before thy face.

This is my hope, my one only consolation, to flee unto thee in every tribulation, to trust in thee, to call upon thee from my inmost heart, and to wait patiently for thy consolation.

A Prayer for mental illumination.

4. O merciful JESUS, enlighten thou me with the brightness of thine inward light, and take away all darkness from the habitation of my heart.

[1] Ps. lxxi. [12].   [2] Isa. xlv. [2, 3].

Repress thou my many wandering thoughts, and break in pieces those temptations which so violently assault me.

Fight thou strongly for me, and vanquish these evil beasts, these alluring desires of the flesh, that so peace may be obtained by thy power, and that thine abundant praise may resound in a holy temple —that is, in a pure conscience.

Command the winds and tempests ; say unto the sea, Be still ; [1] say to the north wind, Blow not ; and there shall be a great calm.

5. Send out thy light and thy truth,[2] that they may shine upon the earth ; for until thou enlighten me, I am but as earth without form and void.

Pour forth thy grace from above, steep my heart in thy heavenly dew, supply fresh streams of devotion to water the face of the earth, that it may bring forth fruit good and excellent.

Lift thou up my mind which is pressed down by a load of sins, and draw up my whole desire to things heavenly ; that having tasted the sweetness of heavenly happiness, it may be irksome to me even to think of earthly things.

6. Do thou pluck me away, and deliver me from all the unlasting comfort of creatures ; for no created thing can fully comfort and quiet my desires.

Join thou me to thyself with an inseparable band of love ; for thou, even thou alone, dost satisfy him that loveth thee, and without thee all things are vain and empty.

[1] Matt. viii. [26].   [2] Ps. xliii. [3].

CHAPTER XXIV.

Of Avoiding Curious Inquiry into the Lives of Others.

MY son, be not curious, nor trouble thyself with idle cares.[1]

What is this or that to thee ? follow thou me.[2]

For what is it to thee whether that man be such or such, or whether this man do or speak this or that ?

Thou shalt not need to answer for others, but shalt give account for thyself ;[3] why, therefore, dost thou thus entangle thyself ?

Behold, I know every one, and do see all things that are done under the sun ; also I understand how it is with every one, what he thinks, what he wishes, and at what his intentions aim.

Unto me, therefore, all things are to be committed ; but do thou keep thyself in peace, and leave the unquiet to be as unquiet as they will.

Whatsoever they shall have done or said shall come upon themselves, for me they cannot deceive.

2. Be not careful for the shadow of a great name, or for the familiar friendship of many, or for the particular and separate affection of men.

For these things both distract the heart and greatly darken it.

Willingly would I speak my word, and reveal my secrets unto thee, if thou wouldst diligently watch for my coming, and open unto me the door of thine heart

[1] Ecclus. iii. [23] ; 1 Tim. v. [13].   [2] John xxi. [22].
[3] Gal. vi. [4, 5].

thou circumspect, and watchful in prayer,
in all things humble thyself.

CHAPTER XXV.

Wherein Firm Peace of Heart and True Spiritual Progress consisteth.

My son, I have said, "Peace I leave with you, my peace I give unto you : not as the world giveth, give I unto you."[1]

Peace is what all desire, but all do not care for the things that pertain unto true peace.

My peace is with the humble and gentle of heart ; in much patience shall thy peace be.

If thou wilt hear me and follow my voice, thou shalt be able to enjoy much peace.

WHAT then shall I do, Lord ?

In every matter look to thyself, as to what thou doest and what thou sayest ; and direct thy whole attention into this, to please me alone, and neither to desire nor to seek anything besides me.

But of the words or deeds of others judge nothing rashly, neither do thou entangle thyself with things not intrusted unto thee. Thus it may come to pass that thou mayest be little or seldom disturbed.

2. But never to feel any disturbance at all, nor

[1] John xiv. [27].

to suffer any trouble of mind or body, belongs not to this life, but to the state of eternal rest.

Think not, therefore, that thou hast found true peace if thou feel no heaviness ; nor that all is well when thou art vexed with no adversary ; nor that all is perfect if all things be done according to thy desire.

Neither do thou think at all highly of thyself, nor account thyself to be specially beloved, if thou be in a state of great devotion and sweetness ; for it is not by these things that a true lover of virtue is known, nor doth the spiritual progress and perfection of a man consist in these things.

3. WHEREIN then, O Lord, doth it consist ?

IN giving thyself up with all thy heart to the divine will, not seeking thine own interest, either in great matters or in small, either in time or in eternity.

So shalt thou keep one and the same countenance, always giving thanks both in prosperity and adversity, weighing all things in an equal balance.

Be thou so full of courage, and so patient in hope, that when inward comfort is withdrawn thou mayest prepare thy heart to suffer even greater things ; and do not justify thyself, as though thou oughtest not to suffer such and so great afflictions, but justify me in whatsoever I appoint, and cease not to praise my holy name.

Then thou walkest in the true and right way of peace, and thou shalt have a sure hope to see my face again with great delight.

Now if thou attain to the full contempt of thyself, know that thou shalt then enjoy abundance of peace, as great as this thy state of sojourning is capable of.

CHAPTER XXVI.

Of the Excellency of a Free Mind, which is sooner gained by Humble Prayer than by Study.

O LORD, it is the business of a perfect man never to withdraw his mind from attentive thought of heavenly things, and thus to pass amidst many cares without care ; not as one destitute of all feeling, but, by the privilege of a free mind, cleaving to no creature with inordinate affection.

2. I beseech thee, my most gracious God, preserve me from the cares of this life, lest I should be too much entangled therein ; and from the many necessities of the body, lest I should be ensnared by pleasure ; and from whatsoever is an obstacle to the soul, lest, broken with troubles, I should be overthrown.

I speak not of those things which worldly vanity so earnestly desireth, but of those miseries which, as punishments and as the common curse of mortality,[1] do weigh down and hinder the soul of thy servant, that it cannot enter into the freedom of the Spirit so often as it would.

3. O my God, thou sweetness ineffable, turn into

---

[1] Gen. iii. [17] ; Rom. vii. [11].

bitterness for me all that carnal comfort which draws me away from the love of eternal things, and in evil wise allures me to itself by the view of some present good.

Let me not be overcome, O Lord, let me not be overcome by flesh and blood ; [1] let not the world and the brief glory thereof deceive me ; let not the devil and his subtle fraud trip me up.

Give me strength to resist, patience to endure, and constancy to persevere.

Give me, instead of all the comforts of the world, the most sweet unction of thy Spirit ; and, in place of carnal love, pour into my heart the love of thy name.

4. Behold ! meat, drink, clothing, and other necessaries for the support of the body, are burdensome to a fervent spirit.

Grant me to use such refreshments moderately, and not to be entangled with an undue desire of them.

It is not lawful to cast away all things, because nature needs to be sustained ; but to require superfluities and those things that are merely pleasurable, the holy law forbiddeth us, for then the flesh would rebel against the Spirit. Herein, I beseech thee, let thy hand govern me and teach me, that I may not exceed in anything.

[1] Rom. xii. [21].

CHAPTER XXVII.

That it is Love of Self which most hindereth from
the Chiefest Good.

My son, thou oughtest to give all for all, and to be
in nothing thine own.

Know thou that the love of thyself doth hurt thee
more than anything in the world.

According to the love and affection thou bearest
to anything, so doth it cleave unto thee more or less.

If thy love be pure,[1] simple, and well-ordered, thou
shalt be free from bondage.

Do not covet that which it is not lawful for thee
to have.　Do not have that which may hinder thee,
and may deprive thee of inward liberty.

Strange it is that thou committest not thyself
wholly unto me from the bottom of thy heart together with all things thou canst have or desire.

2. Why dost thou consume thyself with vain
grief?[2] why dost thou weary thyself with needless
cares?

Submit to my good will, and thou shalt suffer no
hurt.

If thou seek this or that, and wouldst be here or
there, the better to enjoy thine own profit and pleasure, thou shalt never be at peace, nor free from
trouble of mind.　For in every case somewhat will
be wanting, and in every place there will be some
one to cross thee.

3. It profiteth thee not therefore to obtain and

[1] Matt. vi. [22].　　[2] Ex. xviii. [18]; Micah iv. [9].

multiply any outward things, but rather to despise them, and utterly to root them out from thy heart.

And this thou must understand not only of revenues and wealth, but of seeking after honour also, and of the desire of vain praise, which all must pass away with this world.

No place availeth if the spirit of fervour be wanting, neither shall that peace long continue which is sought from without.[1] If the state of thy heart be destitute of a true foundation—that is, if thou stand not steadfast in me—thou mayest change, but shalt not better thyself.

For when occasion ariseth and is laid hold of, thou wilt find that which thou didst flee from, and yet more.

A Prayer for a clean heart, and heavenly wisdom.

4. STRENGTHEN me, O God, by the grace of thy holy Spirit.[2]

Grant me to be strengthened with might in the inner man,[3] and to empty my heart of all useless care and anguish,[4] so that I be not drawn away with sundry desires of anything whatever, whether mean or precious, but that I look on all things as passing away, on myself also as soon to pass away with them.

For nothing abideth under the sun, where all things are vanity and vexation of spirit.[5] O how wise is he that so considereth them !

5. O Lord, grant me heavenly wisdom,[6] that I may learn above all things to seek and to find thee,

---

[1] Isa. xli. [13]. [2] Ps. li. [12]. [3] Eph. iii. [16].
[4] Matt. vi. [34]. [5] Eccles. i. [14], ii. [1]. [6] Wisd. ix. [4].

above all things to enjoy and to love thee, and to think of all other things as they really are, according to thy wise ordering.

Grant me prudence to avoid him that flattereth me, and to endure patiently him that contradicteth me.

Because it is a great part of wisdom not to be moved with every wind of words,[1] nor to give ear to an evil flatterer ; for thus I shall walk securely in the way which I have begun.

CHAPTER XXVIII.

Against the Tongues of Slanderers.

MY son, take it not grievously if some think ill of thee,[2] and speak that which thou wouldest not willingly hear.

Thou oughtest to be the hardest judge of thyself, and to think no man weaker than thyself.

If thou dost walk spiritually, thou wilt not much weigh fleeting words.

It is no small wisdom to keep silence in an evil time, and in thy heart to turn thyself to me, and not to be troubled by the judgment of men.

2. Let not thy peace depend on the tongues of men, for whether they judge well of thee or ill, thou art not on that account other than thyself.   Where are true peace and true glory ? are they not in me ? [3]

---

[1] Eph. iv. [14].   [2] 1 Cor. iv. [13].   [3] John xvi. [33].

And he that careth not to please men, nor feareth to displease them, shall enjoy much peace.

From inordinate love and vain fear ariseth all disquietness of heart and distraction of the mind.

CHAPTER XXIX.

How that we ought to Call upon God, and to Bless him, when Tribulation is upon us.

BLESSED be thy name, O Lord, for ever ; [1] for that it is thy will that this temptation and tribulation should come upon me.

I cannot escape it, but must needs flee unto thee, that thou mayest help me and turn it to my good.

Lord, I am now in affliction, and it is not well with me, but I am much troubled with the present suffering.

And now, O beloved Father, what shall I say ? [2] I am in a strait ; save thou me from this hour.

Yet therefore came I unto this hour that thou mightest be glorified, when I shall have been greatly humbled, and by thee delivered.

Let it please thee, Lord, to deliver me ; [3] for, wretched that I am, what can I do, and whither shall I go without thee ?

Grant me patience, O Lord, even now in this my strait. Help me, my God, and then I will not fear how grievously soever I be afflicted.

[1] Job. i. [21]; Ps. cxiii. [2]. [2] Matt. xxvi.; John xii. [27].
[3] Ps. xxxvii. [40].

2. And now in these my troubles what shall I say?

Lord, thy will be done![1] I have well deserved to be afflicted and grieved.

Surely I ought to bear it; and O that I may bear it with patience, until the tempest be overpast, and all be well again, or even better!

But thine omnipotent hand is able to take even this temptation from me, and to assuage the violence thereof, that I utterly sink not under it, as oftentimes heretofore thou hast done unto me, O my God, my Mercy!

And the more difficult it is to me, so much the more easy to thee is this change of the right hand of the Most High.

CHAPTER XXX.

Of Craving the Divine Aid, and of Confidence of Recovering Grace.

My son, I am the Lord, that giveth strength in the day of tribulation.[2]

Come thou unto me when it is not well with thee.[3]

This is that which most of all hindereth heavenly consolation, that thou art too slow in turning thyself unto prayer.

For before thou dost earnestly supplicate me, thou seekest in the meanwhile many comforts, and lookest for refreshment in outward things.

And hence it cometh to pass that all doth little

[1] Matt. vi. [10].   [2] Nahum i. [7].   [3] Matt. xi. [28].

profit thee, until thou well consider that I am he who doth rescue them that trust in me ; and that out of me there is neither powerful help, nor profitable counsel, nor lasting remedy.

But do thou, having now recovered breath after the tempest, gather strength again in the light of my mercies ; for I am at hand (saith the Lord) to repair all, not only entirely, but also abundantly and in most plentiful measure.

2. Is there anything hard to me ? or shall I be like unto one that promiseth and performeth not ? [1]

Where is thy faith ? stand firmly and with perseverance ; take courage and be patient ; comfort will come to thee in due time.

Wait, wait, I say, for me : I will come and heal thee.

It is a temptation, this that vexeth thee ; and a vain fear, this that affrighteth thee.

What else doth anxiety about the future bring to thee but sorrow upon sorrow ? " Sufficient for the day is the evil thereof." [2]

It is a vain thing and unprofitable to be either disturbed or pleased about future things, which perhaps will never come to pass.

3. But it is in the nature of man to be deluded with such imaginations ; and it is a sign of a mind as yet weak to be so easily drawn away by the suggestions of the enemy.

For so that he may but delude and deceive thee, he careth not whether it be by true things or by false ; whether he overthrow thee with the love of present things, or the fear of future things.

[1] Matt. xxiii. [35].   [2] Matt. vi. [34].

Let not therefore thy heart be troubled, neither let it be afraid.

Trust in me, and put thy confidence in my mercy.[1]

When thou thinkest thyself furthest off from me, oftentimes I am nearest unto thee.

When thou judgest that almost all is lost, then oftentimes the greatest gain of reward is close at hand.

All is not lost when a thing falleth out against thee.

Thou must not judge according to present feeling, nor so take any grief, or give thyself over to it, from whencesoever it cometh, as though all hopes of escape were quite taken away.

4. Think not thyself wholly left although for a time I have sent thee some tribulation, or even have withdrawn thy desired comfort ; for this is the way to the kingdom of heaven.

And without doubt it is more expedient for thee and for the rest of my servants that ye be exercised with adversities, than that ye should have all things according to your desires.

I know the secret thoughts of thy heart, and that it is very expedient for thy welfare that thou be left sometimes without spiritual enjoyment, lest perhaps thou shouldst be puffed up with thy prosperous estate, and shouldst be willing to please thyself in that which thou art not.

That which I have given I can take away, and can restore it again when I please.

5. When I give it, it is still mine ; when I withdraw

[1] Ps. xci. [1].

it, I take not anything that is thine ; for every good and every perfect gift is mine.[1]

If I send thee affliction, or any cross whatsoever, repine not, nor let thy heart fail thee ; I can quickly succour thee, and turn all thy heaviness into joy.

Nevertheless I am righteous, and greatly to be praised when I deal thus with thee.

6. If thou be wise, and consider this rightly, thou wilt never mourn so dejectedly for any adversity but rather wilt rejoice and give thanks.

Yea, thou wilt account this thine especial joy, that I afflict thee with sorrows and do not spare thee.

" As my Father hath loved me, so have I loved you," [2] said I unto my beloved disciples ; whom doubtless I sent not out to temporal joys, but to great conflicts ; not to honour, but to contempt ; not to idleness, but to labours ; not to rest, but that they should bring forth much fruit with patience. Remember thou these words, O my son !

CHAPTER XXXI.

Of the Contempt of all Creatures, in order to Find out the Creator.

O LORD, I stand much in need of yet greater grace, if it be thy will that I should attain to that state, where neither man nor any creature shall be a hindrance unto me.

[1] James i. [17].   [2] John xv. [9].

For as long as anything holds me back, I cannot freely take my flight to thee.

He desired to fly freely that said, " Oh that I had wings like a dove ! for then would I flee away, and be at rest." [1]

What is more quiet than the single eye ? [2] and who more free than he that desireth nothing upon earth ?

A man ought therefore to mount above all creatures, and perfectly to renounce himself, and to be in a sort of ecstasy of mind, and to see that thou, the Creator of all things, hast nothing amongst creatures like unto thyself.

Unless a man be set free from all creatures, he cannot wholly attend unto divine things.

And therefore are there so few contemplative, for that few can wholly withdraw themselves from things created and perishing.

2. To obtain this there is need of much grace to elevate the soul, and carry it away above itself.

And unless a man be uplifted in spirit, and be freed from all creatures, and wholly united unto God, whatsoever he knoweth and whatsoever he hath is of small account.

A long while shall he be little, and lie grovelling below, whoever he be that esteemeth anything great save the one only infinite eternal Good.

And whatsoever is not God is nothing, and ought to be accounted of as nothing.

There is great difference between the wisdom of a man devout and taught of God, and the knowledge of a man learned and studious.

Far more noble is that learning which floweth

from above from the divine influence, than that
which is painfully gotten by the wit of man.

3. There are many that desire contemplation,
but they endeavour not to practise those things
that are needful thereunto.

A great hindrance it is that men rest in signs and
in the things of sense, and little heed perfect mortification.

I know not what it is, by what spirit we are led,
nor what we pretend, we that seem to be called
spiritual, that we take so much pains, and are so
full of anxiety about transitory and mean things,
and so rarely think of our own inward concernments
with full recollection of mind.

4. Alas! presently, after a slight recollection, we
rush into outward things again, and weigh not our
works with diligent examination.

We heed not where our affections lie, nor bewail
the impurity that is in all our actions.

For " all flesh had corrupted his way," and therefore did the great deluge ensue.[1]

Since, then, the inward affection is much corrupted, the action thence proceeding must needs
be corrupted also—a proof of the absence of all
inward strength.

From a pure heart proceedeth the fruit of a good
life.

5. We ask how much a man has done; but from
what principle he acts is not so diligently considered.

We inquire whether he be courageous, rich,
handsome, skilful, a good writer, a good singer, or
a good labourer; but how poor he is in spirit, how

---

[1] Gen. vi. [12], vii. [21].

patient and meek, how devout and spiritual, is sel·
dom spoken of.

Nature respecteth the outward things of a man,
grace turneth itself to the inward.

The one is often disappointed; the other hath
her trust in God, and so is not deceived.

CHAPTER XXXII.

Of Self-Denial, and Renouncing every Evil Appetite.

MY son, thou canst not possess perfect liberty unless
thou wholly renounce thyself.[1]

They all are but in fetters who merely seek their
own interest, and are lovers of themselves. Covetous are they, curious, wanderers, always seeking
what is soft and delicate, not the things of JESUS
Christ, but oftentimes devising and framing that
which will not continue.

For all that is not of God shall perish.

Keep this short and complete saying : " Forsake
all, and thou shalt find all." Forego desire, and
thou shalt find rest.

Consider this well, and when thou hast fulfilled
it thou shalt understand all things.

2. O LORD, this is not the work of one day, nor
children's sport ; yea, rather in this short word is
included all perfection.

MY son, thou oughtest not to turn back, nor at once

[1] Matt. xvi. [24], xix. [8, 9].

to be cast down when thou hearest of the way of the perfect, but rather to be stirred up to higher things, and at least in longing desire to sigh after them.

I would it were so with thee, that thou wert arrived at this, to be no longer a lover of thyself, but to stand merely at my beck, and at his whom I have appointed a father over thee; then thou shouldst exceedingly please me, and all thy life should pass away in joy and peace.

Thou hast yet many things to part with, which unless thou wholly resign unto me, thou shalt not attain to that which thou desirest.

" I counsel thee to buy of me gold tried in the fire, that thou mayest become rich; " [1] that is, heavenly wisdom, which treadeth under foot all lower things.

Set little by earthly wisdom, and study not to please others or thyself.

3. I said that mean things must be bought with things which among men seem precious and of great esteem.

For true heavenly wisdom doth seem very mean, of small account, and almost forgotten among men, as having no high thoughts of itself, nor seeking to be magnified upon earth. Many indeed praise it with their lips, but in their life they are far from it; yet is it the precious pearl [2] which is hidden from many.

[1] Rev. iii. [18].   [2] Matt. xiii. [46].

CHAPTER XXXIII.

Of Inconstancy of Heart, and of having our Final Intent directed unto God.

MY son, trust not to thy feelings, for whatever they be now, they will quickly be changed towards some other thing.

As long as thou livest, thou art subject to change,[1] even against thy will ; so that thou art at one time merry, at another sad ; at one time quiet, at another troubled ; now devout, now undevout ; now diligent, now listless ; now grave, and now light.

But he that is wise and well instructed in the Spirit standeth fast upon these changing things, not heeding what he feeleth in himself, or which way the wind of instability bloweth, but that the whole intent of his mind may be to the right and the best end.

For thus he will be able to continue one and the same and unshaken, in the midst of so many various events directing continually the single eye of his intent unto me.

2. And the purer the eye of the intent is,[2] with so much the more constancy doth a man pass through the several kinds of storms which assail him.

But in many the eye of a pure intent waxes dim, for it is quickly drawn aside to any pleasurable object which meets it.

For it is rare to find one who is wholly free from all blemish of self-seeking.

So of old the Jews came to Bethany to Martha

[1] Job xiv. [2].　　　　[2] Matt. vi. [22].

and Mary, not for Jesus' sake only, but that they might see Lazarus also.[1]

The eye of our intent therefore is to be purified, that it may be single and right,[2] and is to be directed unto me, beyond all the various earthly objects which come between.

CHAPTER XXXIV.

That God is Precious above all Things, and in all Things, to him that Loveth Him.

" Behold ! my God, and my all." What would I more, and what greater happiness can I desire ?

O sweet and delightful word ! but to him only that loveth the word, not the world nor the things that are in the world.

" My God, and my all ! " To him that understandeth enough is said, and to repeat it again and again is pleasant to him that loveth.

For when thou art present, all things do yield delight ; but when thou art absent, everything becometh irksome.

Thou givest quietness of heart, and much peace, and pleasant joy.

Thou makest us to take delight in all things, and in all to praise thee ; neither can anything please long without thee ; but if it be pleasant and grateful, thy grace must needs be present, and it must be seasoned with the sweetness of thy wisdom.

[1] John xii. [9].   [2] Matt. vi. [22].

2. What will not be pleasant to the taste unto him who hath a true relish for thee?

And to him that hath no relish for thee what can be pleasant?

But the wise men of the world, and they also who relish the things of the flesh, come short of thy wisdom;[1] for in the former is found much vanity, and in the latter death.

But they that follow thee in contempt of worldly things, and mortification of the flesh, are known to be truly wise; for they are brought over from vanity to truth, from the flesh to the Spirit.

These relish God; and what good soever is found in creatures, they wholly refer unto the praise of their Maker.

Great, however, yea, very great is the difference between the sweetness of the Creator and of the creature, of Eternity and of time, of Light uncreated and of the light that receiveth its light therefrom.

3. O thou everlasting Light, surpassing all created lights, dart the beams of thy brightness from above, to pierce all the most inward parts of my heart.

Purify, rejoice, enlighten and enliven my spirit with all the powers thereof, that I may cleave unto thee with abundance of joy and triumph.

O when will that blessed and desired hour come, that thou mayest satisfy me with thy presence, and mayest be unto me all in all?

So long as this is not granted me I shall not have perfect joy.

Still, alas! the old man doth live in me:[2] he is not wholly crucified, he is not perfectly dead.

[1] I Cor. i. [26]; Rom. viii. [5]; I John ii. [16].   [2] Rom. vii.

Still doth he mightily strive against the Spirit, and stirreth up inward wars, and suffereth not the kingdom of my soul to be in peace.

4. But thou that rulest the power of the sea, and stillest the rising of the waves thereof,[1] arise and help me!

Scatter the nations that delight in war,[2] crush thou them in thy might.

Display thy greatness, I beseech thee, and let thy right hand be glorified; for there is no other hope or refuge for me save in thee, O Lord my God.[3]

CHAPTER XXXV.

That there is no Security from Temptation in this Life.

MY son, thou art never secure in this life, but as long as thou livest[4] thou shalt always need spiritual armour.

Thou dwellest among enemies, and art assaulted on the right hand and on the left.[5]

If therefore thou defend not thyself on every side with the shield of patience, thou canst not be long without a wound.

Moreover, if thou fix not thy heart on me with sincere willingness to suffer all things for me, thou wilt not be able to bear the heat of this combat, nor to attain to the palm of the blessed.

[1] Ps. lxxxix. [9].　　[2] Ps. lxviii. [30].　　[3] Ps. xxxi. [14].
[4] Job vii. [1].　　[5] 2 Cor. vi. [7].

Thou oughtest therefore manfully to go through all, and to secure a strong hand against whatsoever withstandeth thee.

For to him that overcometh is manna given, but for the indolent there remaineth much misery.

2. If thou seek rest in this life, how wilt thou then attain to the everlasting rest ?

Dispose not thyself for much rest, but for great patience.

Seek true peace, not in earth, but in heaven ; not in men, nor in any other creature, but in God alone.

For the love of God thou oughtest cheerfully to undergo all things ; that is to say, all labour, grief, temptation, vexation, anxiety, necessity, infirmity, injury, detraction, reproof, humiliation, shame, correction, and contempt.

These help to virtue ; these are the trial of a babe in Christ ; these form the heavenly crown.

I will give an everlasting reward for a short labour, and infinite glory for transitory shame.

3. Thinkest thou that thou shalt always have spiritual consolations at will ?

My saints had not such always, but they had many afflictions, and sundry temptations, and great discomforts.

But in all these they did bear up themselves patiently, and trusted rather in God than in themselves, knowing that the sufferings of this time are not worthy to be compared to the future glory.[1]

Wilt thou have that at once which many after many tears and great labours have hardly obtained ?

[1] Rom. viii. [18].

Wait for the Lord, behave thyself manfully, and be of good courage ;[1] be not faithless, do not leave thy place, but steadily expose both body and soul for the glory of God.

I will reward thee in most plentiful wise ; I will be with thee in every tribulation.

CHAPTER XXXVI.

Against the Vain Judgments of Men.

My son, rest thy heart firmly on the Lord, and fear not the judgment of men, when conscience testifieth of thy dutifulness and innocency.

It is a good and happy thing to suffer in such a way ; nor will this be grievous to a heart which is humble, and which trusteth rather in God than in itself.

The most part of men are given to talk much, and therefore little trust is to be placed in them.

Moreover also, to satisfy all is not possible.

Although Paul endeavoured to please all in the Lord, and made himself all things unto all [2] men, yet with him it was a very small thing that he should be judged of man's judgment.[3]

2. He did for the edification and salvation of others what lay in him, and as much as he was able, yet could he not hinder but that he was sometimes judged and despised by others.

[1] Ps. xxvii. [14].   [2] 1 Cor. ix. [22] ; 2 Cor. iv. [2].
[3] Col. i. ; 1 Cor. iv. [3].

Therefore he committed all to God, who knew all; and with patience and humility he defended himself against unjust tongues, and against such as thought vanities and lies, and spake boastfully whatever they listed.

Sometimes notwithstanding he made answer, lest the weak should be offended by his silence.[1]

3. Who art thou that fearest a mortal man? today he is, and to-morrow he is not seen.[2]

Fear God, and thou shalt not need to shrink from the terrors of men.

What harm can the words or injuries of any man do thee? He hurteth himself rather than thee, nor shall he be able to avoid the judgment of God,[3] whosoever he be.

Do thou have God before thine eyes, and contend not with peevish words.

And if for the present thou seem to be worsted and to suffer shame undeservedly, do not therefore repine, neither do thou by impatience lessen thy crown.[4]

But rather lift thou up thine eyes to me in heaven, who am able to deliver thee from all shame and wrong, and to render to every man according to his works.

[1] Acts xxvi.; Phil. i. [14].   [2] 1 Mac. ii. [62, 63].
[3] Rom. ii. [3]; 1 Cor. xi. [32].   [4] Heb. xii. [1, 2].

CHAPTER XXXVII.

*Of Pure and Entire Resignation for the Obtaining
Freedom of Heart.*

My son, forsake thyself, and thou shalt find me.[1]

Choose not anything, nor appropriate anything whatever to thyself, and thou shalt always be a gainer.

For greater grace shall be added to thee the moment thou hast resigned thyself, and hast not resumed thy claim.

Lord, how often shall I resign myself, and wherein shall I forsake myself?

Always and at every hour; as well in small things as in great. I except nothing, but do desire that thou be found stripped of all things.

Otherwise, how canst thou be mine, and I thine, unless thou be stripped of all self-will, both within and without?

The sooner thou doest this, the better it will be with thee; and the more fully and sincerely thou doest it, so much the more shalt thou please me, and so much the greater shall be thy gain.

2. Some there are who resign themselves, but with exceptions: for they put not their whole trust in God, therefore they study how to provide for themselves.

Some also at first do offer all, but afterwards, being assailed with temptation, they return again

[1] Matt. xvi. [24].

to their own ways, and therefore make no progress in the ways of virtue.

These shall not attain to the true liberty of a pure heart, nor to the favour of my sweetest friendship, unless they first make an entire resignation and a daily oblation of themselves. Without this there neither is nor can be a fruitful union.

3. I have very often said unto thee, and now again I say the same, Forsake thyself,[1] resign thyself, and thou shalt enjoy much inward peace.

Give all for all ; seek nothing, ask back nothing ; abide purely and with a firm confidence in me, and thou shalt possess me ; thou shalt be free in heart, and darkness shall not tread thee down.

Let this be thy whole endeavour, let this be thy prayer, this thy desire—that, being stripped of all selfishness, thou mayest with entire simplicity follow JESUS only, and, dying to thyself, mayest live eternally to me.

Then all vain imaginations, evil perturbations, and superfluous cares shall fly away.

Then also immoderate fear shall leave thee, and inordinate love shall die.

CHAPTER XXXVIII.

Of Good Government of Ourselves in Things Outward, and of Recourse to God in Dangers.

MY son, thou oughtest with all diligence to endeavour that, in every place and action, and in all out-

[1] Matt. xvi. [24].

ward business, thou be inwardly free, and thoroughly master of thyself ; and that all things be under thee, and not thou under them.

Thou must be lord and master of thine own actions, not a servant or a hireling.

Rather shouldest thou be as a freed man and a true Hebrew, passing over into the lot and freedom of the sons of God.

For they stand above things present, and contemplate the things eternal.

They look on transitory things with the left eye, and with the right do behold the things of heaven.

Temporal things cannot draw them to cleave unto them ; rather do they draw temporal things to serve them, and this in such way as they are ordained by God, and are appointed by the great Workmaster, who hath left nothing in his creation without due order.

2. If too thou stand steadfast in all things, and do not estimate what thou seest and hearest by the outward appearance, nor with a carnal eye, but at once in every affair dost enter with Moses into the tabernacle [1] to ask counsel of the Lord, thou shalt sometimes hear the divine oracle, and shalt return instructed concerning many things, both present and to come.

For Moses always had recourse to the tabernacle for the deciding of doubts and questions, and fled to the help of prayer for support under dangers and the iniquity of men.

So oughtest thou in like manner to fly to the closet of thine heart,[2] very earnestly craving the divine favour.

[1] Ex. xxxiii. [9].   [2] Matt. vi. [6].

For we read that for this cause Joshua and the children of Israel were deceived by the Gibeonites because they asked not counsel at the mouth of the Lord,[1] but, giving credit too lightly to their fair words, were deluded by their counterfeit piety.

CHAPTER XXXIX.

That a Man should not be Over-careful in Matters of Business.

My son, always commit thy cause to me ; I will dispose well of it in due time. Wait for my ordering of it, and thou shalt find it will be for thy good.

O Lord, I do most cheerfully commit all unto thee, for my care can little avail.

Would that I did not so much dwell on future things, but gave myself up without a struggle to thy good pleasure.

2. My son, oftentimes a man vehemently struggleth for somewhat he desireth, and when he hath arrived at it he beginneth to be of another mind ; for man's affections do not long continue fixed on one object, but rather do urge him from one thing to another.

It is therefore no small benefit for a man to forsake himself even in the smallest things.

3. The true profiting of a man consisteth in the

[1] Josh. ix. [14].

denying of himself ; and he that thus denieth himself, liveth in great freedom and security.

But the old enemy,[1] who always setteth himself against all that are good, ceaseth at no time from tempting, but day and night lieth grievously in wait, to cast the unwary, if he can, headlong into the snare of deceit.

Therefore, " Watch ye, and pray," saith our Lord, " that ye enter not into temptation." [2]

CHAPTER XL.

That Man hath of himself no Good Thing, nor Anything whereof he can Glory.

" LORD, what is man, that thou art mindful of him ? or the son of man, that thou visitest him ? " [3]

What hath man deserved that thou shouldest grant him thy favour ?

O Lord, what cause have I to complain if thou forsake me ? or if thou do not that which I desire, what can I justly say against it ?

Surely this I may truly think and say, Lord, I am nothing, I can do nothing, I have nothing that is good of myself, but in all things I am wanting, and do ever tend to nothing.

And unless thou help me, and inwardly instruct me, I must become altogether lukewarm and careless.

2. But thou, O Lord, art always the same, and

---

[1] 1 Peter v. [8].   [2] Matt. xxvi. [41].
[3] Ps. viii. [4].

endurest for ever ; [1] always good, just, and holy ;
doing all things well, justly, and holily, and disposing
all things with wisdom.

But I, that am more ready to go backward than
forward, do not ever continue in one estate, for
" seven times are passed over me." [2]

Yet is it soon better with me, when it so pleaseth
thee, and when thou vouchsafest to stretch forth thy
helping hand ; for thou canst help me alone without
human aid, and canst so strengthen me that my
countenance shall be no more changed, but my heart
shall be turned to thee alone, and be at rest.

3. Wherefore, if I could once perfectly cast off
all human comfort, either for the attainment of devotion, or because of mine own necessities enforcing
me to seek after thee (because that no mortal man
could comfort me), then might I well hope in thy
grace, and rejoice for the gift of fresh consolation.

4. Thanks be unto thee, from whom all things
proceed, whensoever it is well with me.

But I am in thy sight mere vanity and nothing,
a man weak, and never continuing in one stay.

Whereof then can I glory ? or for what do I
desire to be respected ? is it for that I am nothing ?
yet this is most vain.

Mere empty glory is in truth an evil pest, a very
great vanity ; because it draweth a man from true
glory, and robbeth him of heavenly grace.

For whilst he pleaseth himself, he displeaseth
thee ; whilst he gapeth after the praise of men, he
is deprived of true virtues.

5. But the true glory and holy exultation is for a

---

[1] Ps. cii. [12].   [2] Dan. iv. [10, 23, 32].

man to glory in thee,[1] and not in himself; to rejoice in thy name, not in his own strength, and not to delight in any creature but for thy sake.

Praised be thy name, not mine; magnified be thy work, not mine. Let thy holy name be blessed, but to me let no part of men's praises be given.[2]

Thou art my glory, thou art the joy of my heart.

In thee will I glory and rejoice all the day; but as for myself, I will not glory, but in my infirmities.

6. Let the Jews seek honour one of another,[3] I will seek that which cometh from God alone.

For all human glory, all temporal honour, all worldly height, compared to thy eternal glory, is vanity and folly.

O my God, my Truth, and my Mercy, O Blessed Trinity, to thee alone be praise, honour, power, and glory, for ever and ever.

CHAPTER XLI.

Of the Contempt of all Temporal Honour.

MY son, trouble not thyself if thou see others honoured and advanced, whilst thou art contemned and debased.

Lift up thy heart into heaven to me, and the contempt of men on earth shall not grieve thee.

LORD, we are blind, and are quickly misled by vanity.

---

[1] Hab. iii. [18].   [2] Ps. cxiii. [3], cxv. [1].   [3] John v. [14].

If I look rightly into myself, I cannot say that any creature hath ever done me wrong ; and therefore I cannot justly complain before thee.

2. But because I have often and grievously sinned against thee, all creatures do justly take arms against me.

Unto me, therefore, shame and contempt are justly due ; but unto thee praise, honour, and glory.

And unless I prepare myself with cheerful willingness to be despised and forsaken of all creatures, and to be esteemed altogether nothing, I cannot obtain inward peace and stability, nor be spiritually enlightened, nor be fully united unto thee.

CHAPTER XLII.

That our Peace is not to be Set on Men.

My son, if thou rest thy peace on any one because of the opinion which thou hast of him, or because of thine intimate acquaintance with him, thou shalt ever be inconstant and inthralled.

But if thou have recourse unto the ever-living and abiding Truth, the departure or death of a friend shall not grieve thee.

Thy regard for thy friend ought to be grounded in me ; and for my sake is he to be beloved, whosoever he be that thou thinkest well of, and who is very dear unto thee in this life.

Without me friendship hath no strength and no

continuance ; neither is that love true and pure which is not knit by me.

Thou oughtest to be so dead to such affections towards thy friends, that (as much as appertaineth unto thee) thou shouldest be willing to be without all human friendship.

Man approacheth so much the nearer unto God the further he departeth from all earthly comfort.

And the lower he descendeth in himself, and the meaner he becometh in his own sight, the higher he ascendeth towards God.

But he that attributeth any good unto himself, hindereth the entry of God's grace ; for the grace of the Holy Spirit ever seeketh an humble heart.[1]

If thou knewest perfectly to annihilate thyself, and to empty thyself of all created love, then should I be constrained to flow into thee with great abundance of grace.

When thou hast regard unto creatures, the sight of the Creator is withdrawn from thee.

Learn in all things to overcome thyself, for the love of thy Creator, and then shalt thou be able to attain to divine knowledge.

How small soever anything be, if it be inordinately loved and regarded, it keepeth thee back from the highest good, and defileth the soul.

[1] I Peter v. [5].

CHAPTER XLIII.

Against Vain and Secular Knowledge.

MY son, let not the sayings of men move thee, however fair and ingenious they may be. " For the kingdom of God consisteth not in word, but in power." [1]

Observe well my words, for they inflame the heart and enlighten the mind; they cause compunction, and carry with them many a consolation.

Never read the Word of God in order to appear more learned or more wise.

Be studious for the mortification of thy sins; for this will profit thee more than the knowledge of many difficult questions.

2. When thou shalt have read and known many things, thou oughtest ever to return to the one beginning and principle.

I am he that teacheth man knowledge; and I give unto little children a clearer understanding than can be taught by man.

He therefore to whom I speak shall quickly be wise, and shall profit much in the Spirit.

Woe be to them that inquire many curious things of men, and little care about the way of serving me !

The time will come when the Master of masters shall appear, Christ the Lord of angels, to hear the lessons of all ; that is, to examine the consciences of every one.

And then will he search Jerusalem with candles ;

[1] 1 Cor. iv. [20]

and the hidden things of darkness shall be laid open,[1] and the arguing of men's tongues shall be silent.

3. I am he who in one instant doth raise up the humble mind, so that a man shall understand more reasonings of eternal truth than if he had studied ten years in the schools.

I teach without noise of words, without confusion of opinions, without the desire of honour, without bandying of arguments.

I am he who instructeth men to despise earthly things, to loathe things present, to seek things heavenly, to relish things eternal, to flee honours, to endure offences, to place all hope in me, out of me to desire nothing, and above all things ardently to love me.

4. A certain one, by loving me entirely, became instructed in divine things, and was wont to speak that which was admirable.

He profited more by forsaking all things than by studying subtilties.

But to some men I speak common things, to others things uncommon ; to some I appear sweetly by signs and figures, but to some I reveal mysteries with much light.

The voice of books is indeed one, but it instructs not all alike ; for I am the teacher of the truth within, I am the searcher of the heart, the discerner of the thoughts, the mover of actions, distributing to every man as I judge meet.

[1] Zeph. i. [12] ; 1 Cor. iv. [5].

CHAPTER XLIV.

Of not Attracting to Ourselves Outward Things.

MY son, in many things it is thy duty to be ignorant, and to esteem thyself as dead upon earth, and as one to whom the whole world is crucified.[1]

Thou must also pass by many things with a deaf ear, and rather think of those which belong unto thy peace.

It is more useful to turn away one's eyes from unpleasing things, and to leave every one to his own opinion, than to be a slave to contentious discourses.

If all stand well betwixt thee and God, and if thou hast his judgment in thy mind, thou shalt the more easily endure to be overcome.

2. O LORD, to what a pass are we come ! Behold, we bewail a temporal loss : for a pitiful gain we toil and run ; and the spiritual losses of our soul are forgotten, and hardly at last return to the memory.

That which little or nothing profiteth we heed, and that which is especially necessary we slightly pass over : because the whole man doth slide off into outward things ; and unless he speedily repent, he settleth down in them, and that willingly.

[1] Gal. vi. [14].

CHAPTER XLV.

That Credit is not to be given to All ; and that Man is prone to Offend in Words.

GRANT me help, O Lord, in tribulation, for vain is the help of man ! [1]

How often have I been deceived, finding want of faithfulness where I thought myself sure !

And how often have I found it where beforehand I least expected it !

It is in vain therefore to trust in men ; but the salvation of the righteous is of thee, O God !

Blessed be thou, O Lord my God, in all things that befall us.

We are weak and unstable ; we are quickly deceived, and soon changed.

2. Who is he that is able in all things so warily and circumspectly to keep himself as never to fall into any deceit or perplexity ?

But he that trusteth in thee, O Lord, and seeketh thee with a single heart, doth not so easily fall. [2]

And if he do fall into any tribulation, be he ever so much entangled, yet he shall quickly either through thee be delivered, or by thee be comforted ; for thou wilt not forsake him that trusteth in thee, even to the end.

A friend is rarely to be found that continueth faithful in all his friend's distresses.

Thou, O Lord, even thou alone, art most faithful at all times, and there is none like unto thee.

[1] Ps. lx. [11].   [2] Prov. x. [29].

7

3. O how wise was that holy soul that said, " My mind is firmly settled and grounded in Christ."

If it were so with me, then would not human fear easily vex me, nor the darts of words move me.

Who can foresee all things ? who is able to beware beforehand of evils to come ? If things even foreseen do oftentimes hurt us, how can things unlooked for do otherwise than wound us grievously ?

But wretched that I am, why did I not provide better for myself ? why also have I so easily trusted others ?

But we are men, nothing else but frail men, although by many we may be reputed and called angels.

To whom shall I give credit, O Lord ? to whom but to thee ? thou art the truth, which neither doth deceive nor can be deceived.

And, on the other side, " every man is a liar," [1] weak, inconstant, and subject to fall, especially in words ; and therefore we must not immediately give credit to that which in the outward show seemeth at the first to sound aright.

4. O with what wisdom hast thou warned us to beware of men ; and because a man's foes are they of his own household,[2] not forthwith to believe if one should say, Lo here, or, Lo there.

My hurt has been my instructor, and O that I might thereby increase my caution and not my folly.

" Be wary," saith one, " be wary, keep to thyself what I tell thee ; " and whilst I hold my peace, and think it is secret, he cannot himself keep that which

[1] Rom. iii. [4].   [2] Micah vii. [6].

he desired me to keep, but presently betrayeth both me and himself, and is gone.

From such tales and such indiscreet persons protect me, O Lord, that I neither fall into their hands, nor ever commit such things myself.

Grant me to observe truth and constancy in my words, and remove far from me a crafty tongue.

What I am not willing to suffer in others, I ought by all means to avoid myself.

5. O how good is it, and how it tendeth to peace, to be silent about other men, and not to believe at random all that is said, nor eagerly to report what we have heard.[1]

How good it is to lay one's self open to few, and always to be seeking after thee who art the searcher of the heart.[2]

Nor should we be carried about with every wind of words, but we should desire that all things, both within and without, be accomplished according to the pleasure of thy will.

How safe is it, for the keeping of heavenly grace, to avoid appearances, and not to seek those things that seem to cause admiration abroad, but to follow with all diligence the things which bring amendment of life, and zeal.

6. To how many hath virtue itself, known and over hastily commended, been hurtful!

How profitable hath grace been when preserved in silence in this frail life, which is temptation and warfare!

[1] Prov. xxv. [9].   [2] Isa. xxvi. [3].

CHAPTER XLVI.

Of Putting our Trust in God when Evil Words arise.

MY son, stand steadily, and put thy trust in me :[1]
for what are words but words ?

They fly through the air, but hurt not the rock.

If thou be guilty, see that thou be willing to
amend thyself ; if conscience reproach thee not,
resolve to suffer willingly for God's sake.

It is but a small matter to suffer sometimes a few
words, if thou hast not yet the courage to endure
hard stripes.

And why do such small matters go to thy heart,
but because thou art yet carnal, and regardest men
more than thou oughtest ?

For because thou art afraid to be despised, therefore thou art not willing to be reproved for thy
faults, but seekest the shelter of excuses.

2. But look better into thyself, and thou shalt
acknowledge that the world is yet alive in thee,
and a vain desire to please men.

For when thou shunnest to be abased and reproved
for thy faults, it is evident that thou art neither
truly humble nor truly dead to the world, nor the
world crucified to thee.

But give diligent ear to my words, and thou
shalt not regard ten thousand words spoken by
men.

Behold, if all should be spoken against thee that
could be most maliciously invented, what would it
hurt thee if thou sufferedst it to pass entirely away.

[1] Ps. xxxvii. [3].

and madest no more reckoning of it than of a mote ?
could it pluck so much as one hair from thy head ? [1]

3. But he that hath no heart within him, and hath
not God before his eyes, is easily moved with a word
of dispraise.

Whereas he that trusteth in me, and hath no wish
to trust in his own judgment, shall be free from the
fear of men.

For I am the judge [2] and the discerner of all
secrets : I know how the matter was ; I know him
that offered the injury, and him that suffered it.

From me hath this proceeded ; this hath happened by my permission, that the thoughts of many
hearts might be revealed.[3]

I shall judge the guilty and the innocent ; but
by a secret judgment I would beforehand prove
them both.

4. The testimony of men oftentimes deceiveth ;
but my judgment is true ; it shall stand, and not
be overthrown.

It is commonly hidden, and not known in all
respects, but to few : notwithstanding it never
erreth, neither can it err, although to the eyes of
the foolish it seemeth not right.

Men ought therefore to have recourse to me
in every judgment, and not to lean on their own
opinion.

For the just man will not be moved,[4] whatsoever befalleth him from God ; and if any unjust
charge be brought against him, he will not be much
troubled.

---

[1] Matt. x. [30] ; Luke xii. [7].   [2] Ps. vii. [8].
[3] Luke ii. [35].   [4] Prov. xii. [13].

Neither will he rejoice with a foolish exultation if by means of others he be reasonably vindicated.

For he considereth that I am he that searcheth the heart and reins,[1] and judgeth not according to the outside, nor according to human appearance.

For that oftentimes in my sight is found worthy of blame which in the judgment of men is thought to be commendable.

5. O LORD GOD, the just judge, strong and patient, thou who knowest the frailty and wickedness of men, be thou my strength, and all my trust, for mine own conscience sufficeth me not.

Although I know nothing against myself,[2] yet I cannot hereby justify myself; for without thy mercy, in thy sight shall no man living be justified.[3]

CHAPTER XLVII.

That all Grievous Things are to be Endured for the sake of Eternal Life.

MY son, be not dismayed by the painful labours which thou hast undertaken for me, neither be thou utterly cast down because of any tribulations which befall thee; but let my promise strengthen and comfort thee in all events.

I am able to reward thee above all measure and degree.

Thou shalt not long toil here, and shalt not always be oppressed with grief.

[1] Ps. vii. [9]; Rev. ii. [23].　　[2] 1 Cor. iv. [4].　　[3] Ps. cxliii. [2].

Wait a little while, and thou shalt see a speedy end of thine evils.

There will come an hour when all labour and trouble shall cease.

Poor and brief is all that which passeth away with time.

2. Do with thy might what thou doest; labour faithfully in my vineyard; [1] I will be thy reward.

Write, read, mourn, keep silence, pray, suffer crosses manfully; life everlasting is worthy of all these, yea, and of greater combats.

Peace shall come in the day which is known unto the Lord, and it shall be neither day nor night, [2] such as now is, but everlasting light, infinite brightness, steadfast peace, and secure rest.

Then thou shalt not say, " Who shall deliver me from the body of this death? " [3] nor cry, " Woe is me, that I sojourn in Mesech! " [4] for death shall be cast down headlong, and there shall be salvation which cannot fail : there shall be no more anxious thoughts, but blessed joy, sweet and lovely company.

3. O if thou hadst seen the everlasting crowns of the saints in heaven, [5] and with how great glory they now rejoice who in times past were contemptible to this world, and esteemed unworthy of life itself, truly thou wouldst presently humble thyself even unto the dust, and wouldst rather seek to be under the feet of all than to have command so much as over one.

Neither wouldst thou desire the pleasant days of this life, but rather wouldst rejoice to suffer

[1] Matt. xx. [7].   [2] Zech. xiv. [7].   [3] Rom. vii. [24].
[4] Ps. cxx. [5].   [5] Wisd. iii. [1–9], v. [16].

affliction for God, and esteem it thy greatest gain to be reputed as nothing amongst men.

4. O if thou hadst a relishing of these things, and didst suffer them to sink into the bottom of thy heart, how couldst thou so much as once complain ?

Are not all painful labours to be endured for the sake of life eternal ?

It is no small matter to lose or to gain the kingdom of God.

Lift up thy face therefore unto heaven ; behold, I and all my saints with me, who in this world had great conflicts, do now rejoice, are now comforted, now secure, now at rest, and they shall remain with me everlastingly in the kingdom of my father.

CHAPTER XLVIII.

Of the Day of Eternity, and this Life's Straitnesses.

O MOST blessed mansion of the city which is above ! [1] O most clear day of eternity, which night obscureth not, but the highest truth ever enlighteneth ! O day ever joyful, ever secure, and never changing into a contrary state !

Oh that that day would once appear, and that all these temporal things were at an end !

To the saints it shineth, glowing with everlasting brightness ; but to those that are pilgrims on the earth it appeareth only afar off, and as it were through a glass.

[1] Rev. xxi. [2].

2. The citizens of heaven do know how joyful that day is; but the banished children of Eve bewail the bitterness and tediousness of this.

The days of this life are short and evil,[1] full of sorrow and straitnesses.

Here a man is defiled with many sins, ensnared with many passions, held fast by many fears, racked with many cares, distracted with many curiosities, entangled with many vanities, compassed about with many errors, worn with many labours, burdened with temptations, enervated by pleasures, tormented with want.

3. Oh, when shall these evils be at an end? when shall I be delivered from the miserable bondage of my sins?[2] when shall I be mindful, O Lord, of thee alone?[3] when shall I fully rejoice in thee?

When shall I enjoy true liberty without any hindrances, without any trouble of mind and body?

When shall I have solid peace, peace secure and undisturbed, peace within and peace without, peace every way assured?

O merciful JESU, when shall I stand to behold thee? when shall I contemplate the glory of thy kingdom? when wilt thou be unto me all in all?

O when shall I be with thee in thy kingdom, which thou hast prepared for thy beloved from all eternity?

I am left, a poor and banished man, in the land of mine enemies, where there are daily wars and great calamities.

---

[1] Job vii. [2] Rom. vii. [24]. [3] Ps. lxxi. [16].

4. Comfort my banishment, assuage my sorrow: for my whole desire sigheth after thee.

For all is burdensome to me, whatsoever this world offereth for my consolation.

I long to enjoy thee in my inmost soul, but I cannot attain unto it.

My desire is that I may be wholly given up to things heavenly, but temporal things and unmortified passions weigh me down.

With the mind I wish to be above all things, but with the flesh I am enforced against my will to be beneath all.

Thus, unhappy man that I am,[1] I fight against myself, and am become grievous to myself, whilst my spirit seeketh to be above, and my flesh to be below.

5. O what do I inwardly suffer, whilst in my mind I dwell on things heavenly, and presently in my prayers a multitude of carnal fancies rise up to me! O my God, be not thou far from me, nor turn away in wrath from thy servant.[2]

Cast forth thy lightning and disperse them; shoot out thine arrows, and let all the imaginations of the enemy be confounded.

Gather in and call home my senses unto thee; make me to forget all worldly things; enable me to cast away speedily, and to despise all the imaginations of wickedness.

Succour me, O thou the everlasting Truth, that no vanity may move me.

Come to me, thou heavenly sweetness, and let all impurity flee from before thy face.

[1] Rom. vii. [24], viii. [23].   [2] Ps. lxxi. [12].

Pardon me also, and in mercy deal gently with me, as often as in prayer I think on aught beside thee.

I must truly confess that I am wont to be subject to many distractions.

For oftentimes I am not there where I stand or sit, but rather I am there whither my thoughts do carry me.

Where my thoughts are, there am I; and commonly there are my thoughts where my affection is.

That too readily occurs to me which is by nature delightful or by custom is pleasing.

6. And for this cause, thou that art truth itself hast plainly said, "Where thy treasure is, there will thy heart be also." [1]

If I love heaven, I willingly muse on heavenly things.

If I love the world, I rejoice at the felicity of the world, and grieve for the adversity thereof.

If I love the flesh, I shall fancy oftentimes those things that are pleasing to the flesh.

If I love the Spirit, I shall delight to think on things spiritual.

For whatsoever I love, thereof do I willingly speak and hear, and carry home with me the images thereof.

But blessed is the man [2] who for thy sake, O Lord, is willing to part with all creatures, who does violence to his nature, and through fervour of the Spirit crucifieth the lusts of the flesh; that so with a serene conscience he may offer pure prayers unto thee, and, all earthly things both outwardly and inwardly being excluded, he may be meet to be admitted into the angelical choirs.

[1] Matt. vi. [21].   [2] Matt. xix.

CHAPTER XLIX.

Of the Desire of Everlasting Life, and how great Rewards are Promised to those that Strive Resolutely.

My son, when thou perceivest the desire of everlasting bliss to be given thee from above, and longest to depart out of the tabernacle of this body, that thou mayest contemplate my brightness without shadow of turning, open thy heart wide, and receive this holy inspiration with thy whole desire.

Give greatest thanks to the Heavenly Goodness, which treateth thee with such condescension, visiting thee mercifully, stirring thee up fervently, powerfully sustaining thee, lest through thine own weight thou fall down to earthly things.

Neither dost thou obtain this by thine own thought or endeavour, but by the mere condescension of heavenly grace and divine favour; to the end that thou mayest make further progress in all virtue, and obtain greater humility, and prepare thyself for future conflicts, and endeavour to cleave unto me with the whole affection of thy heart, and to serve me with fervent willingness.

2. My son, oftentimes the fire burneth, but the flame ascendeth not up without smoke.

So likewise the desires of some men burn towards heavenly things, and yet they are not free from the temptations of carnal affection.

And therefore it is not altogether purely for the honour of God that they make such earnest requests to him.

Such also oftentimes are thy desires, which thou hast pretended to be so serious and earnest.

For those desires are not pure and perfect which are tainted with self-love.

3. Ask not for that which is delightful and profitable to thee, but for that which is acceptable to me, and which tendeth to my honour ; for if thou judgest aright, thou oughtest to prefer and follow my appointment rather than thine own desire, or anything whatever that is to be desired.

I know thy desire, and have heard thy frequent groanings.

Now thou longest to enjoy the glorious liberty of the sons of God ; now dost thou delight in the everlasting habitation, thy heavenly home full of joy : but that hour is not yet come ; there still remaineth another time, and that a time of war,[1] a time of labour and of trial.

Thou desiredst to be filled with the chiefest good, but thou canst not attain it yet.

I AM he ; wait thou for me (saith the Lord) until the kingdom of God shall come.

4. Thou art still to be tried upon earth, and to be exercised in many things.

Comfort shall be sometimes given thee, but the abundant fulness thereof shall not be granted.

Take courage therefore, and be valiant,[2] as well in doing as in suffering things contrary to nature.

It is thy duty to put on the new man,[3] and to be changed into another man.

It is thy duty oftentimes to do what thou

---

[1] Job vii. [1].   [2] Josh. i. [7].   [3] Eph. iv. [24].

wouldst not; thy duty to leave undone what thou wouldst do.

That which pleaseth others shall go well forward; that which pleaseth thee shall not speed.

That which others say shall be heard; what thou sayest shall be accounted nothing : others shall ask and shall receive; thou shalt ask but shalt not obtain.

5. Others shall be great in the praise of men, but about thee there shall be no word.

To others this or that shall be committed, but thou shalt be accounted a thing of no use.

At this nature will sometimes be troubled, and it is a great thing if thou bear it with silence.

In these and many such like things the faithful servant of the Lord is wont to be tried, how far he can deny and break his will in all things.

There is scarcely anything wherein thou hast such need to die to thyself, as in seeing and suffering those things that are contrary to thy will; especially when that is commanded to be done which seemeth unto thee inconvenient or useless.

And because thou being under authority darest not resist the higher power, therefore it seems hard to thee to walk at another's beck, and to feel that thou must give up all thine own will.

6. But consider, my son, the fruit of these labours, the end near at hand, and the reward exceeding great, and thou wilt not grudge to bear them; rather thou wilt have the strongest comfort of thy patience.

For instead of that little of thy will which now thou so readily forsakest, thou shalt always have thy will in heaven.

Yea, there thou shalt find all that thou canst wish, all that thou shalt be able to desire.

There thou shalt have within thy reach all good, without fear of losing it.

There shall thy will be ever one with me; it shall not covet any outward or selfish thing.

There none shall withstand thee, no man shall complain of thee, no man hinder thee, nothing come in thy way; but all things thou canst desire shall be there altogether present, and shall refresh thy whole affection, and fill it up to the brim.

There I will give thee glory for the reproach which here thou sufferedst, the garment of praise for heaviness, for the lowest place a kingly throne for ever.

There shall the fruit of obedience appear, the labour of repentance shall rejoice, and humble subjection shall be gloriously crowned.

7. At present then bend thyself humbly under all, and care not who said this or commanded it.

But take especial care, that whether thy superior, or thine inferior, or thine equal, require anything of thee, or do but insinuate their desire, thou take it all in good part, and with a sincere will endeavour to fulfil it.

Let one seek this, another that; let this man glory in this, the other in that, and be praised a thousand thousand times; but do thou rejoice neither in this, nor in that, but in the contempt of thyself, and in the good pleasure and honour of me alone.

This is what thou art to wish, that, whether it be by life or by death, God may be always glorified in thee.

CHAPTER L.

How the Desolate ought to Give up Himself into
the Hands of God.

O LORD God, holy Father, be thou blessed both
now and for evermore, because as thou wilt so is
it done, and what thou doest is good.

Let thy servant rejoice in thee, not in himself
nor in anything else ; for thou alone art the true
gladness, thou art my hope and my crown, thou
art my joy and my honour, O Lord.

What hath thy servant but what he hath received
from thee,[1] even without any merit of his ?

Thine are all things, both what thou hast given
and what thou hast made.

I am poor, and in trouble, from my youth ;[2] and
sometimes my soul is sorrowful even unto tears ;
sometimes also it is disturbed within itself by reason
of sufferings which hang over me.

2. I long after the joy of peace, the peace of thy
children I earnestly crave, who are fed by thee in
the light of thy comfort.

If thou give peace, if thou pour into my heart
holy joy, the soul of thy servant shall be full of
melody, and shall become devout in thy praise.

But if thou withdraw thyself (as many times
thou dost), he will not be able to run the way of
thy commandments ; but rather he will bow his
knees, and smite his breast, because it is not now
with him as it was in times past, when thy candle
shined upon his head, and under the shadow of thy

[1] I Cor. iv. [7].   [2] Ps. lxxxviii. [15].

wings he was protected from the temptations which assaulted him.

3. O righteous Father, and ever to be praised, the hour is come that thy servant is to be proved.

O beloved Father, meet and right it is that in this hour thy servant should suffer somewhat for thy sake.

O Father, evermore to be honoured, the hour is come which from all eternity thou didst foreknow should come, that for a short time thy servant should outwardly be oppressed, but inwardly should ever live with thee ;

That he should be for a little while despised, and humbled, and in the sight of men should fail, and be wasted with sufferings and languors,—that he might rise again with thee in the morning dawn of the new light, and be glorified in heaven.

Holy Father, thou hast so appointed it, and so wilt have it ; and that is fulfilled which thyself hast commanded.

4. For this is a favour to thy friend, that for love of thee he may suffer and be afflicted in the world, how often soever and by whom soever thou permittest such trials to befall him.

Without thy counsel and providence, and without cause, nothing cometh to pass in the earth.

It is good for me, Lord, that thou hast humbled me,[1] that I may learn thy righteous judgments, and may cast away all haughtiness of heart and all presumption.

It is profitable for me that shame hath covered my face, that I may seek to thee for consolation rather than to men.

[1] Ps. cxix. [71].

I have learned also hereby to dread thine unsearchable judgments, who afflictest the just with the wicked, though not without equity and justice.

5. I give thee thanks, for that thou hast not spared my sins, but hast worn me down with bitter stripes, inflicting sorrows and sending anxieties upon me within and without.

There is none else under heaven who can comfort me, but thou only, O Lord my God, the heavenly physician of souls, who woundest and healest, who bringest down to hell and bringest back again.[1]

Thy discipline shall be over me, and thy rod itself shall instruct me.

6. Behold, O beloved Father, I am in thy hands, I bow myself under the rod of thy correction.

Strike my back and my neck too, that my crookedness may be conformed to thy will.

Make me a dutiful and humble disciple of thine (as thou hast been wont to do me good), that I may be ready at every beck of thy divine pleasure.

Unto thee I commend myself and all mine to be corrected: it is better to be punished here than hereafter.

Thou knowest all and everything, and there is nothing in the conscience of man which can be hidden from thee.

Before anything is done, thou knowest that it will come to pass, and hast no need that any should teach thee or admonish thee of those things which are being done on the earth.

Thou knowest what is expedient for my spiritual

[1] Tobit xiii. [2] ; Ps. xviii. [16].

progress, and how greatly tribulation serves to scour off the rust of my sins.

Do with me according to thy good pleasure, and disdain me not for my sinful life, known to none so thoroughly and clearly as to thee alone.

7. Grant me, O Lord, to know that which is worth knowing, to love that which is worth loving, to praise that which pleaseth thee most, to esteem that highly which to thee is precious, to abhor that which in thy sight is filthy and unclean.

Suffer me not to judge according to the sight of the eyes, nor to give sentence according to the hearing of the ears of ignorant men ; but with a true judgment to discern between things visible and spiritual, and above all to be ever searching after the good pleasure of thy will.

8. The minds of men are often deceived in their judgments ; the lovers of the world too are deceived in loving only things visible.

What is a man ever the better for being esteemed great by man ?

The deceitful in flattering the deceitful, the vain man in extolling the vain, the blind in commending the blind, the weak in magnifying the weak, deceiveth him ; and in truth doth rather put him to shame, while he so vainly praiseth him.

For what every one is in thy sight, that is he, and no more.

CHAPTER LI.

*That a Man ought to Employ himself in Works of
Humility, when Strength is wanting for Higher
Employment.*

MY son, thou art not able always to continue in the
more fervent desire of virtue, nor to persist in the
higher pitch of contemplation ; but thou must needs
sometimes, by reason of original corruption, descend
to inferior things, and bear the burden of this corruptible life, though against thy will, and with
wearisomeness.

As long as thou carriest a mortal body thou shalt
feel weariness and heaviness of heart.

Thou oughtest therefore in the flesh oftentimes
to bewail the burden of the flesh ; for that thou
canst not employ thyself unceasingly in spiritual
studies and divine contemplation.

2. Then it is expedient for thee to flee to humble
and outward works, and to refresh thyself with good
actions ; to await with a firm confidence my coming
and heavenly visitation, to bear patiently thy banishment and the dryness of thy mind, till I shall again
visit thee, and set thee free from all anxieties.

For I will cause thee to forget thy painful toils,
and to enjoy thorough inward quietness.

I will spread open before thee the pleasant fields
of Holy Scripture, that with an enlarged heart thou
mayest begin to run the way of my commandments.

And thou shalt say, " The sufferings of this present
time are not worthy to be compared with the glory
that shall be revealed in us." [1]

[1] Rom. viii. [18].

CHAPTER LII.

That a Man ought not to account himself as Worthy of Comfort, but rather as Deserving of Chastisement.

O LORD, I am not worthy of thy consolation, nor of any spiritual visitation; and therefore thou dealest justly with me when thou leavest me poor and desolate.

For though I could shed a sea of tears, still I should not be worthy of thy consolation.

I am not then worthy of anything but to be scourged and punished, because I have grievously and often offended thee, and in many things have greatly sinned.

Wherefore, all things duly considered, I am not worthy even of the least comfort.

But thou, O gracious and merciful God, who willest not that thy works should perish, to show the riches of thy goodness upon the vessels of mercy, vouchsafest even beyond all his desert to comfort thy servant above the manner of men.

For thy consolations are not like to the discourses of men.

2. What have I done, O Lord, that thou shouldst bestow any heavenly comfort upon me?

I remember not that I have done any good, but that I have been always prone to sin and slow to amendment.

This is true, and I cannot deny it. If I should say otherwise, thou wouldst stand against me,[1] and there would be none to defend me.

---

[1] Job ix. [2, 3].

What have I deserved for my sins but hell and everlasting fire?

I confess in very truth that I am worthy of all scorn and contempt, nor is it fit that I should be remembered amongst thy devout servants.

And although I be unwilling to hear this, yet notwithstanding, for the truth's sake, I will lay open my sins against myself, that so the more readily I may be counted worthy to obtain thy mercy.

3. What shall I say, in that I am guilty and full of all confusion?

My mouth can utter nothing but this word only, " I have sinned, O Lord! I have sinned;[1] have mercy on me, pardon me."

Spare me a little, that I may bewail my griefs, before I go into the land of darkness, a land covered with the shadow of death.[2]

What dost thou so much require of a guilty and miserable sinner as that he be contrite, and that he humble himself for his offences?

Of true contrition and humbling of the heart ariseth hope of forgiveness; the troubled conscience is reconciled; the favour of God, which was lost, is recovered; man is preserved from the wrath to come; and God and the penitent soul meet together with a holy kiss.

4. Humble contrition for sins is an acceptable sacrifice unto thee, O Lord,[3] savouring much sweeter in thy presence than the perfume of frankincense.

This is also the pleasant ointment [4] which thou

---

[1] Ps. li.   [2] Job x. [21].
[3] Ps. li. [17].   [4] Luke vii. [38].

wouldst to be poured upon thy sacred feet ; for a contrite and humbled heart thou never hast despised.[1]

Here is the place of refuge from the angry face of the enemy ; here is amended and washed away whatever defilement and pollution hath been anywhere contracted.

CHAPTER LIII.

That the Grace of God is not given to those who relish Earthly Things.

MY son, my grace is precious ; it suffereth not itself to be mingled with outward things, nor with earthly consolations.

Thou oughtest therefore to cast away all hindrances to grace, if thou desire to receive the inpouring thereof.

Choose, therefore, a secret place to thyself, love to live alone with thyself, desire the conversation of none ; but rather pour out devout prayer unto God, that thou mayest keep thy soul contrite and thy conscience pure.

Esteem thou the whole world as nothing ; prefer attendance upon God before all outward things.

For thou wilt not be able to attend upon me, and at the same time to take delight in things transitory.

Thou oughtest to remove thyself away from thine

[1] Ps. li. [17].

acquaintance and friends,[1] and not to depend on any temporal comfort.

So the blessed apostle Peter beseecheth that the faithful of Christ would keep themselves in this world as strangers and pilgrims.[2]

2. O how great a confidence shall he have at the hour of death whom no affection to any earthly thing detaineth in the world.

But the having a heart so retired from all, the unspiritual mind doth not as yet comprehend; nor doth the carnal man know the liberty of him that is spiritual.

Notwithstanding, if he desire to be truly spiritual, he ought to renounce those who are far off as well as those who are near unto him, and to beware of no man more than of himself.

If thou perfectly overcome thyself, thou shalt very easily bring all else under the yoke.

The perfect victory is, to triumph over ourselves.

For he that keepeth himself subject, in such sort that his affections be obedient to reason, and his reason in all things obedient to me, he truly is conqueror of himself and lord of the world.

3. If thou desire to mount unto this height, thou must set out courageously, and lay the axe to the root, that thou mayest pluck up and destroy both that hidden inordinate inclination to self and all love of private and earthly good.

On this sin almost all dependeth, whatsoever is thoroughly to be overcome; which evil being once vanquished and subdued, there will presently ensue great peace and tranquillity.

[1] Matt. xix. [29].   [2] I Peter ii. [11].

But because few labour perfectly to die unto themselves, or altogether to go out of themselves, therefore in themselves they remain entangled, nor can be lifted up in spirit above themselves.

But for him that desireth to walk freely with me, it is necessary that he mortify all his corrupt and inordinate affections, and that he do not earnestly cleave to any creature with particular love.

CHAPTER LIV.

Of the Different Stirrings of Nature and Grace.

My son, mark diligently the stirrings of nature and grace ; for in a very contrary yet subtile manner do they move, so that they can hardly be distinguished but by him that is spiritually and inwardly enlightened.

All men indeed desire that which is good, and pretend some good in their words and deeds ; and therefore, under the show of good, many are deceived.

Nature is crafty, and seduceth many, ensnareth and deceiveth them, and always proposeth herself for her end and object :

But Grace walketh in simplicity, abstaineth from all show of evil, sheltereth not herself under deceits, doeth all things purely for God's sake, in whom also she finally resteth.

2. Nature is unwilling and loath to die, or to be kept down, or to be overcome, or to be in subjection, or readily to be subdued :

But Grace studieth self-mortification, resisteth sensuality, seeketh to be in subjection, is desirous to be kept under, and wisheth not to use her own liberty. She loveth to be kept under discipline, and desireth not to rule over any, but always to live and remain and be under God, and for God's sake is ready humbly to bow down unto all.

Nature striveth for her own advantage, and considereth what profit she may reap by another.

Grace considereth not what is profitable and convenient unto herself, but rather what may be for the good of many.

Nature willingly receiveth honour and reverence.

Grace faithfully attributeth all honour and glory unto God.

3. Nature feareth shame and contempt.

Grace rejoiceth to suffer reproach for the name of JESUS.

Nature loveth leisure and bodily ease.

Grace cannot be unemployed, but cheerfully embraceth labour.

Nature seeketh to have things that are curious and beautiful, and abhorreth those which are cheap and coarse.

Grace delighteth in what is plain and humble, despiseth not rough things, and refuseth not to be clothed in that which is old and worn.

Nature respecteth temporal things, rejoiceth at earthly gain, sorroweth for loss, is irritated by every little injurious word.

Grace looketh to things eternal, cleaveth not to things temporal, is not disturbed at losses, nor soured with hard words; because she hath placed her treasure and joy in heaven, where nothing of it perisheth.

4. Nature is covetous, doth more willingly receive than give, and loveth to have things private and her own.

Grace is kind of heart, and ready to share with others, shunneth private interest, is content with a little, judgeth that it is more blessed to give than to receive.[1]

Nature inclineth a man to the creature, to his own flesh, to vanities, and to wandering hither and thither.

Grace draweth him unto God and to every virtue, renounceth the creature, avoideth the world, hateth the desires of the flesh, restraineth wanderings abroad, blusheth to be seen in public.

Nature is willing to have some outward solace, whereby she may receive delight of the senses.

Grace seeketh consolation in God alone, and to have delight in the highest good, above all visible things.

5. Nature turneth everything to her own gain and profit, she cannot bear to do anything without reward; but for every kindness she hopeth to obtain either what is equal or what is better, or at least praise or favour; and is very earnest to have her works and gifts much valued.

Grace loveth even her enemies, and is not puffed up with multitude of friends; and thinketh not greatly of high birth, unless it be joined with more exalted virtue.

Grace seeketh no temporal thing, nor desireth any other reward save God alone, and asketh not more

[1] Acts xx. [35].

of temporal necessaries than what may serve her for the obtaining of things eternal.

6. Nature rejoiceth to have many friends and kinsfolk, she glorieth of noble place and noble birth ; she smileth on the powerful, fawneth upon the rich, applaudeth those who are like herself.

Grace favoureth the poor rather than the rich, sympathizeth more with the innocent than with the powerful, rejoiceth with the true man, not with the deceitful.

She is ever exhorting good men to strive for the best gifts, and by all virtue to become like to the Son of God.

Nature quickly complaineth of want and of trouble.

Grace endureth need with firmness and constancy.

7. Nature referreth all things to herself, striveth and argueth for herself.

Grace bringeth back all to God, from whence originally they proceed ; she ascribeth no good to herself, nor doth she arrogantly presume ; she contendeth not, nor preferreth her own opinion before others ; but in every matter of sense and understanding she submitteth herself unto the eternal wisdom and the divine judgment.

Nature is eager to know secrets and to hear news ; she loveth to appear abroad and to make proof of many things by her own senses ; she desireth to be acknowledged, and to do things for which she may be praised and admired.

Grace careth not to hear news, nor to understand curious matters (because all this taketh its rise from the old corruption of man), seeing that upon earth there is nothing new, nothing durable.

Grace teacheth therefore to restrain the senses, to shun vain complacency and ostentation, humbly to hide those things that are worthy of admiration and praise, and from every thing and in every knowledge to seek profitable fruit, and the praise and honour of God.

She will not have herself nor that which pertaineth to her publicly praised, but desireth that God should be blessed in his gifts, because that of mere love he bestoweth all things.

8. This grace is a supernatural light, and a certain special gift of God, and the proper mark of the elect, and a pledge of everlasting salvation. It raiseth up a man from earthly things to love the things of heaven, and from being carnal maketh him a spiritual man.

The more therefore nature is depressed and subdued, so much the more is grace infused, and every day by new visitations the inward man is created anew according to the image of God.

CHAPTER LV.

Of the Corruption of Nature, and the Efficacy of Divine Grace.

O LORD my God, who hast created me after thine own image and likeness,[1] grant me this grace, which thou hast showed to be so great and so necessary to salvation ; that I may overcome my most evil nature, which draweth me to sin and to perdition.

[1] Gen. i. [26].

For I feel in my flesh the law of sin contradicting the law of my mind,[1] and leading me captive to the obeying of sensuality in many things ; neither can I resist the passions thereof, unless thy most holy grace, being infused into my heart, do assist me.

2. There is need of thy grace, O Lord, and of large supplies thereof, that nature may be overcome, which is ever prone to evil from her youth.[2]

For through Adam the first man, nature being fallen and corrupted by sin, the penalty of this stain hath descended upon all mankind, in such sort that " nature " itself, which by thee was created good and upright, is now taken for the sin and infirmity of corrupted nature ; because the inclination thereof left unto itself draweth to evil and to lower things.

For the small power which remaineth is, as it were, a spark lying hid in the ashes.

This is natural reason itself, encompassed about with great darkness, yet still retaining power to discern the difference between true and false, good and evil ; although it be unable to fulfil all that it approveth, and enjoyeth no longer the full light of the truth, nor soundness in its own affections.

3. Hence it is, O my God, that I delight in thy law after the inward man,[3] knowing thy commandment to be good, just, and holy, reproving also all evil and sin, as things to be avoided.

But with the flesh I serve the law of sin, in that I obey my senses rather than my reason.

Hence it is that to will what is good is present with me, but how to perform it I find not.

Hence it is that I often purpose many good things,

[1] Rom. vii. [23].   [2] Gen. viii. [21].   [3] Rom. vii. [22].

but because grace is wanting to help my infirmity, upon a light resistance I start back and faint.

Hence it cometh to pass that I know the way of perfection, and see clearly enough what I ought to do ; but being pressed down by the weight of mine own corruption, I rise not to that which is more perfect.

4. O Lord, how entirely needful is thy grace for me, to begin any good work, to go on with it, and to accomplish it.

For without that grace I can do nothing,[1] but in thee I can do all things, when thy grace doth strengthen me.

O grace heavenly indeed ! without which our most worthy actions are nothing, nor are any gifts of nature to be esteemed.

Neither arts nor riches, beauty nor strength, wit nor eloquence, are of any value before thee, without thy grace, O Lord.

For gifts of nature are common to good and bad, but the peculiar gift of the elect is grace or love ; and they that bear this honourable mark are accounted worthy of everlasting life.

So eminent is this grace that neither the gift of prophecy, nor the working of miracles, nor any speculation, how high soever, is of any esteem without it.

No, not even faith, nor hope, nor any other virtues, are unto thee acceptable without charity and grace.[2]

5. O most blessed grace, that makest the poor in spirit rich in virtues, and renderest him who is rich in many goods humble in heart !

Come thou down unto me, come and replenish me

[1] John xv. [5].   [2] I Cor. xiii. [13].

early with thy comfort, lest my soul faint for weariness and dryness of mind.

I beseech thee, O Lord, that I may find grace in thy sight ; for thy grace is sufficient for me, though other things that nature desireth be not obtained.

Although I be tempted and vexed with many tribulations, yet I will fear no evil,[1] so long as thy grace is with me.

This alone and by itself is my strength ; this alone giveth advice and help.

This is stronger than all enemies, and wiser than all the wise.

6. Thy grace is the mistress of truth, the teacher of discipline, the light of the heart, the solace in affliction, the driver away of sorrow, the expeller of fear, the nurse of devotion, the mother of tears.

Without this, what am I but a withered branch and an unprofitable stock, only meet to be cast away !

Let thy grace therefore, O Lord, always prevent and follow me, and make me to be continually given to good works, through thy Son JESUS Christ. Amen.

CHAPTER LVI.

That we ought to Deny Ourselves and Imitate Christ by the Cross.

MY son, the more thou canst go out of thyself, so much the more wilt thou be able to enter into me.

[1] Ps. xxiii. [4].

As to desire no outward thing produceth inward peace, so the forsaking of ourselves inwardly joineth us unto God.

I will have thee learn perfect resignation of thyself to my will, without contradiction or complaint.

Follow thou me: "I AM the way, the truth, and the life." [1] Without the way, there is no going; without the truth, there is no knowing; without the life, there is no living. I AM the way, which thou oughtest to follow; the truth, which thou oughtest to trust; the life, which thou oughtest to hope for.

I AM the way inviolable, the truth infallible, the life that cannot end.

I AM the straightest way, the highest truth, the true life, the blessed life, the life uncreated.

If thou remain in my way, thou shalt know the truth, and the truth shall make thee free, and thou shalt lay hold on eternal life.

2. If thou wilt enter into life, keep the commandments. [2]

If thou wilt know the truth, believe me.

If thou wilt be perfect, sell all. [3]

If thou wilt be my disciple, deny thyself utterly. [4]

If thou wilt possess a blessed life, despise this life present.

If thou wilt be exalted in heaven, humble thyself in this world. [5]

If thou wilt reign with me, bear the cross with me. [6]

For only the servants of the cross can find the way of blessedness and of true light.

---

[1] John xiv. [6].   [2] Matt. xix. [17].   [3] Matt. xix. [21].
[4] Luke ix. [23].   [5] John xii. [25].   [6] Luke xiv. [27].

8

3. O Lord JESUS, forasmuch as thy life was narrow and despised by the world, grant me to imitate thee, though the world despise.

For the servant is not greater than his Lord,[1] nor the disciple above his Master.

Let thy servant be exercised in thy life, for therein consisteth my salvation and my true holiness.

Whatsoever I read or hear besides it doth not give me full refreshment or delight.

4. MY son, inasmuch as thou knowest and hast read all these things, happy shalt thou be if thou do them.

"He that hath my commandments, and keepeth them, he it is that loveth me; and I will love him, and will manifest myself unto him,"[2] and will make him sit together with me in my Father's kingdom.

O LORD JESU, as thou hast said and promised, so let it come to pass, and grant that I may not be wholly undeserving of this favour.

I have received the cross from thy hand; I have borne it, and will bear it even unto death, even as thou hast laid it upon me.

Verily the life of a Christian is a cross, yet is it also a guide to paradise.

I have begun, I may not go back, neither is it fitting to leave that which I have undertaken.

5. Courage then, brethren, let us go forward together! JESUS will be with us.

For the sake of JESUS we have undertaken this cross; for the sake of JESUS let us persevere in the cross.

[1] Matt. x. [24]; Luke vi. [40].   [2] John xiv. [21].

He will be our helper, who is also our guide and forerunner.

Behold, our King entereth in before us, and he will fight for us.

Let us follow manfully, let no man fear any terrors; let us be prepared to die valiantly in battle, nor bring shame on our glory by flying from the cross.

CHAPTER LVII.

That a Man should not be too much Dejected, even when he Falleth into some Defects.

MY son, patience and humility in adversity are more pleasing to me than much comfort and devotion in prosperity.

Why art thou so grieved for every little matter spoken against thee?

Although it had been much more, thou oughtest not to have been moved.

But now let it pass; it is not the first that hath happened, nor is it anything new; neither shall it be the last, if thou live long.

Thou art courageous enough so long as nothing adverse befalleth thee.

Thou canst give good counsel also, and canst strengthen others with thy words; but when any tribulation suddenly cometh to thy door, thou failest in counsel and in strength.

Observe then thy great frailty, of which thou too often hast experience in small matters.

It is notwithstanding intended for thy good, when these and such like trials happen to thee.

2. Put it out of thy heart as well as thou canst ; and if it touch thee, yet let it not cast thee down, nor long perplex thee.

At least bear it patiently, if thou canst not bear it joyfully.

Although thou be unwilling to hear it, and conceive indignation thereat, yet restrain thyself, and suffer no ill-advised word to pass out of thy mouth, whereby Christ's little ones may be offended.

The storm which is now raised shall quickly be appeased, and inward grief shall be sweetened by the return of grace.

I yet live, saith the Lord, and am ready to help thee,[1] and to give thee greater comfort than before, if thou put thy trust in me, and call devoutly upon me.

3. Be more patient of soul, and gird thyself to greater endurance.

All is not lost, although thou feel thyself very often afflicted or grievously tempted.

Thou art a man, and not God ; thou art flesh, not an angel.

How canst thou look to continue alway in the same state of virtue, when an angel in heaven hath fallen, as also the first man in paradise ? [2]

I am he who lifteth up the mourners in safety and soundness ; and those that know their own weakness I advance to mine own divine glory.

4. O LORD, blessed be thy word, more sweet unto my mouth than honey and the honey-comb.[3]

---

[1] Isa. xlix. [18].   [2] Gen. iii.   [3] Ps. cxix. [103].

What should I do in these so great tribulations and straits, unless thou didst comfort me with thy holy words?

What matter is it how much or what I suffer, so I may at length attain to the haven of salvation?

Grant me a good end, grant me a happy passage out of this world.

Be mindful of me, O my God, and direct me in the right way to thy kingdom.   Amen.

CHAPTER LVIII.

That High Matters and God's Secret Judgments are not to be Narrowly Inquired into.

MY son, beware thou dispute not of high matters, nor of the secret judgments of God: why this man is so left, and that man taken into such great favour; why also one man is so much afflicted, and another so greatly advanced.

These things are beyond the reach of man, neither is it in the power of any reason or disputation to search out the judgments of God.

When therefore the enemy suggesteth these things unto thee, or some curious people raise the question, let thy answer be that of the prophet, " Thou art just, O Lord, and thy judgment is right." [1]

And again, " The judgments of the Lord are true and righteous altogether." [2]

My judgments are to be feared, not to be discussed;

[1] Ps. cxix. [137].   [2] Ps. xix. [9].

for they are such as cannot be comprehended by the understanding of man.

2. In like manner I advise thee not to inquire, nor dispute of the merits of holy men, which of them is holier than the other, or which shall be the greater in the kingdom of heaven.

These things oftentimes breed strife and unprofitable contentions,[1] they also nourish pride and vainglory; from whence spring envy and dissensions, whilst one will proudly prefer this, and the other another.

To desire to know and search out such things answereth no good end, and is painful to righteous souls ; for I am not the God of dissension, but of peace ; which peace consisteth rather in true humility than in self-exaltation.

3. Some are carried with zeal of affection towards these or those ; but this is rather human love than divine.

I am he who made all the saints ; I gave them grace ; I obtain for them glory.

I know what every one hath deserved ; I have prevented them with the blessings of my goodness.

I foreknew my beloved ones before the beginning of the world.

I chose them out of the world ; they chose not me first.[2]

I called them by grace, I drew them by mercy, I led them safely through sundry temptations.

I have poured into them glorious consolations, I give them perseverance, I crown their patience.

4. I acknowledge both the first and the last ; I embrace all with love inestimable.

[1] 2 Tim. ii. [14].   [2] John xv. [16].

I am to be praised in all my saints ; I am to be blessed above all things, and to be honoured in every one whom I have thus gloriously exalted and pre-destinated, without any merits of their own.

He therefore that despiseth one of the least of mine,[1] honoureth not the greatest ; for that I made both the small and the great.[2]

And he that dispraiseth any of my saints dis-praiseth me also, and all the rest in the kingdom of heaven.

These all are one through the bond of love ; their thought is the same, their will is the same, and they all love one another.

5. But still (which is a far higher thing) they love me more than themselves or any merits of their own.

For being ravished above self and self-love, they are wholly carried out to love me, in whom also they rest with full fruition.

Nothing can turn them back, nothing can press them down ; for being full of the eternal Truth, they burn with the fire of unquenchable charity.

Let therefore carnal and natural men, who can love nothing but their own selfish joys, forbear to dispute of the state of God's saints. Such men add and take away according to their own fancies, not as it pleaseth the eternal Truth.

6. Many are ignorant, especially those who are but little enlightened ; and these can seldom love any with a perfect spiritual love.

They are as yet much drawn by a natural affection and human friendship to this man or to that. And according to the experience they have of themselves

[1] James ii. [1–5].　　　[2] Wisd. vi. [7].

in their earthly affections, so do they frame imaginations of things heavenly.

But there is an incomparable distance between the things which the imperfect imagine and the things which they that are enlightened are enabled to behold through revelation from above.

7. Beware therefore, my son, that thou handle not with vain curiosity things which exceed thy knowledge ; [1] but rather let this be thy great business and endeavour, to attain if it be but the meanest place in the kingdom of God.

Even if any man should know who exceeds another in sanctity, or who is accounted the greatest in the kingdom of heaven ; what would this wisdom profit him, unless he should humble himself the more in my sight, and then should rise up to give the greater praise to my name, in proportion to this his knowledge ?

Far more acceptable to God is he that thinketh of the greatness of his own sins, and the smallness of his virtues, and how far he is from the perfection of saints, than he who disputeth of their greatness or littleness.

8. They are well, yea right well, contented, if men would but content themselves, and refrain from vain discourses.

They glory not of their own merits, inasmuch as they ascribe no goodness to themselves, but attribute all to me, who of mine infinite love have given them all things.

They are filled with so great love of God, and with such an overflowing joy, that there is no glory

[1] Ecclus. iii. [21].

nor happiness that is or that can be wanting unto them.

All the saints, the higher they are in glory, the more humble are they in themselves, and the nearer and dearer unto me.

And therefore it is written, " That they did cast their crowns before God, and fell down on their faces before the Lamb, and adored him that liveth for ever and ever." [1]

9. Many inquire, who is the greatest in the kingdom of God, who know not whether they shall ever be numbered among the least.

It is a great thing to be even the least in heaven, where all are great ; for they all shall be called, and shall be, the sons of God.

" The least shall become a thousand," [2] and " the sinner of an hundred years shall die." [3]

For when the disciples asked who should be the greatest in the kingdom of heaven, they received such an answer as this :

" Except ye be converted, and become as little children, ye shall not enter into the kingdom of heaven : whosoever therefore shall humble himself as this little child, the same is greatest in the kingdom of heaven." [4]

10. Woe be unto them who disdain to humble themselves willingly with little children ; because the low gate of the kingdom of heaven will not give them entrance.[5]

Woe also to the rich, who have here their consolation ; for whilst the poor enter into the

---

[1] Rev. iv. [10]. [2] Isa. lx. [22]. [3] Isa. lxv. [20].
[4] Matt. xviii. [3]. [5] Matt. vii. [14].

kingdom of God, they shall stand lamenting without.

Rejoice, ye that be humble ;[1] and ye poor, be ye filled with joy : for yours is the kingdom of God, if at least ye walk according to the truth.

CHAPTER LIX.

That all our Hope and Trust are to be Fixed in God alone.

LORD, what is my confidence which I have in this life ? or what is the greatest comfort I can derive from anything under heaven ?

Is it not thou, O Lord my God, whose mercies are without number ?

Where hath it ever been well with me without thee ? or when could it be ill with me, when thou wert present ?

I had rather be poor for thy sake, than rich without thee.

I rather choose to be a pilgrim on earth with thee, than without thee to possess heaven. Where thou art, there is heaven ; and where thou art not, there is death and hell.

Thou art all my desire, and therefore I must needs sigh and call and earnestly pray unto thee.

For I have none fully to trust to, none that can seasonably help me in my necessities, but only thee, my God.

[1] Matt. v. [3].

Thou art my hope, thou my confidence ; thou art my comforter, and in all things most faithful unto me.

2. All men seek their own gain.[1] Thou settest forward my salvation and my profit only, and turnest all things to my good.

Although thou exposest me to divers temptations and adversities, yet thou orderest all this to mine advantage, who art wont to try thy beloved ones in a thousand ways.

In which trial of me thou oughtest no less to be loved and praised, than if thou didst fill me full of heavenly consolations.

3. In thee, therefore, O Lord God, I place my whole hope and refuge ; on thee I rest in my tribulation and anguish : for I find all to be weak and inconstant, whatsoever I behold save in thee.

For many friends cannot profit, nor strong helpers assist, nor prudent counsellors give a profitable answer, nor the books of the learned afford comfort, nor any precious substance deliver, nor any place, however retired and lovely, give shelter, unless thou thyself dost assist, help, strengthen, console, instruct, and guard us.

4. For all things, that seem to belong to the attainment of peace and felicity, without thee are nothing, and do bring in truth no felicity at all.

Thou therefore art the end of all that is good, the height of life, the depth of all that can be spoken ; and to hope in thee above all things is the strongest comfort of thy servants.

To thee, therefore, do I lift up mine eyes ; in thee, my God, the Father of mercies, do I put my trust.

[1] Phil. ii. [21].

Bless and sanctify my soul with thy heavenly blessings, that it may become thy holy habitation, and the seat of thine eternal glory ; and let nothing be found in this temple of thy dignity which shall offend the eyes of thy majesty.

According to the greatness of thy goodness and the multitude of thy mercies look upon me, and hear the prayer of thy poor servant, who is exiled far from thee in the land of the shadow of death.

Protect and keep the soul of me, the meanest of thy servants, amidst the many dangers of this corruptible life ; and by thy grace accompanying direct me along the way of peace to the land of everlasting light. *Amen.*

THE FOURTH BOOK.
CONCERNING THE COMMUNION.

THE FOURTH BOOK.

CONCERNING THE COMMUNION.

A Devout Exhortation to the Holy Communion.

"COME unto me, all ye that labour and are heavy laden, and I will refresh you,"[1] saith the Lord.

"The bread which I will give is my flesh, which I will give for the life of the world."[2]

"Take ye and eat ; this is my body, which is given for you :[3] do this in remembrance of me."[4]

"He that eateth my flesh and drinketh my blood dwelleth in me, and I in him."

"The words which I have spoken unto you are spirit and life."[5]

CHAPTER I.

With how great Reverence Christ ought to be Received.

THESE are thy words, O Christ, the everlasting Truth, though not spoken all at one time, nor written in one place.

[1] Matt. xi. [28].   [2] John vi. [51].   [3] Matt. xxvi. [26].
[4] 1 Cor. xi. [24].   [5] John vi. [56, 63).

Because therefore they are thine, and true, they are all thankfully and faithfully to be received by me.

They are thine, and thou hast pronounced them ; and they are mine also, because thou hast spoken them for my salvation.

I cheerfully receive them from thy mouth, that they may be the more deeply implanted in my heart.

They arouse me, those most gracious words, so full of sweetness and of love ; but mine own offences do dishearten me, and an impure conscience driveth me back from the receiving of so great mysteries.

The sweetness of thy words doth encourage me, but the multitude of my sins weigheth me down.

2. Thou commandest me to come confidently unto thee, if I would have part with thee ; and to receive the food of immortality, if I desire to obtain everlasting life and glory.

" Come unto me (sayest thou), all ye that labour and are heavy laden, and I will refresh you." [1]

O sweet and loving word in the ear of a sinner, that thou, my Lord God, shouldst invite the poor and needy to the participation of thy most holy body and blood !

But who am I, Lord, that I should presume to approach unto thee ?

Behold, the heaven of heavens cannot contain thee, and thou sayest, " Come ye all unto me."

3. What meaneth this so gracious a condescension and this so loving invitation ?

How shall I dare to come, who know not any good in myself, whereupon I may presume ?

[1] Matt. xi. [28].

How shall I bring thee into my house, I that have so often offended thy most gracious countenance?

Angels and archangels stand in awe of thee: holy and righteous men do fear thee: and sayest thou, "Come ye all unto me"?

Unless thou, O Lord, didst say this, who would believe it to be true?

And unless thou didst command it, who could attempt to draw near?

Behold, Noah that just man laboured a hundred years in the making of the ark,[1] that he might be saved with a few; and how can I in one hour's space prepare myself to receive with reverence the maker of the world?

4. Moses, thy great servant, and thine especial friend, made an ark of incorruptible wood, which also he covered over with the finest gold, wherein to lay up the tables of the law;[2] and I, a corrupted creature, how shall I dare so unconcernedly to receive the maker of the law and the giver of life?

Solomon, the wisest of the kings of Israel, bestowed seven years in building a magnificent temple to the praise of thy name.[3]

He also celebrated the feast of dedication thereof eight days together; he offered a thousand peace-offerings, and he solemnly set the ark of the covenant in the place prepared for it with the sound of trumpets and great joy.[4]

And I, the most miserable and poorest of men, how shall I bring thee into my house, I that can scarce spend one half-hour in true devotion? And

[1] Gen. vi. [2].
[2] Ex. xxv. [10–16].
[3] I Kings vi. [38].
[4] I Kings viii.

would that I could even once spend something like one half-hour in worthy and due manner !

5. O my God, how earnestly did they study and endeavour to please thee !

Alas, how little is that which I do ! how short a time do I spend when I am preparing myself to receive the communion !

Seldom am I wholly collected ; very seldom indeed am I cleansed from all distraction.

And yet surely in the life-giving presence of thy Godhead no unbecoming thought ought to intrude itself, nor should any creature occupy my heart ; for it is not an angel, but the Lord of angels, whom I am about to entertain.

6. And yet very great is the difference between the ark of the covenant with its relics, and thy most pure body with its unspeakable virtues ; between those legal sacrifices, figures of things to come, and the true sacrifice of thy body, the fulfilment of all ancient sacrifices.

Why therefore am I not more ardent and zealous in seeking thine adorable presence ?

Why do I not prepare myself with greater solicitude to receive thy holy things ? whereas those holy ancient patriarchs and prophets, yea, kings also and princes, with the whole people, showed such an affectionateness of devotion to thy divine service.

7. The most devout king David danced before the ark of God with all his might,[1] calling to mind the benefits bestowed in time past upon his forefathers. He made instruments of sundry kinds, he set forth psalms, and appointed them to be sung

[1] 2 Sam. vi. [14].

with joy; he also oftentimes himself sung to the harp, being inspired with the grace of the Holy Ghost. He taught the people of Israel to praise God with their whole hearts, and with voices full of harmony to bless and praise him every day.

If so great devotion was then used, and such celebrating of divine praise was kept up before the ark of the testament, what reverence and devotion ought now to be preserved by me and all Christian people, during the ministration of this sacrament, in receiving the most precious body and blood of Christ.

8. Many run to divers places to visit the memorials of saints departed, are full of admiration at hearing of their deeds, behold with awe the spacious buildings of their temples, and find their affections moved by whatever is connected with their memory.

But, behold, thou art thyself here present with me on thine altar, my God, Saint of saints, Creator of men, and Lord of the angels.

Often, in looking after such memorials, men are moved by curiosity, and by the novelty of fresh sights, whilst little or no fruit of amendment is carried home; particularly when they go from place to place with levity, without a true penitent heart.

But here, in this holy sacrament, thou art wholly present, my God, the man Christ JESUS: here, to all worthy and devout receivers, is granted an abundant fruit of eternal salvation.

There is here to attract men nothing that savours of levity, of curiosity, or of sense; nothing but firm faith, devout hope, and sincere charity.

9. O God, the invisible Creator of the world, how wonderfully dost thou deal with us; how sweetly

and graciously dost thou dispose of all things with thine elect, to whom thou offerest thyself to be received in this sacrament !

For this verily exceedeth all understanding. This specially draweth the hearts of the devout, and inflameth their affections.

For even thy true faithful ones, who dispose their whole life to amendment, by this most precious sacrament oftentimes gain much of the grace of devotion and love of virtue.

10. O the admirable and hidden grace of this sacrament, which only the faithful ones of Christ do know. But the unbelieving and such as are slaves unto sin cannot have experience thereof.

In this sacrament spiritual grace is conferred, and the strength which was lost is restored in the soul, and the beauty which by sin had been disfigured again returneth.

This grace is sometimes so great, that out of the fulness of devotion here given, not the mind only, but the weak body also, feeleth great increase of strength bestowed on it.

11. Nevertheless our coldness and negligence is much to be bewailed and pitied, that we are not drawn with greater affection to receive Christ, in whom doth consist all the hope of those that are to be saved, and all their merit.

For he himself is our sanctification and redemption ; he himself is the comfort of those who are here but travellers, and the everlasting fruition of saints.

It is therefore much to be lamented that many do so little consider this salutary mystery, which causeth joy in heaven, and preserveth the whole world.

Alas for the blindness and hardness of man's heart, that doth not more deeply weigh so unspeakable a gift ; but rather cometh by the daily use thereof to regard it little or nothing !

12. For if this most holy sacrament were to be celebrated in one place only, and consecrated by one only priest in the world, with how great desires dost thou think would men be affected to that place, and toward such a priest of God, that they might be witnesses of the celebration of these divine mysteries ?

But now many are made priests, and in many places Christ is offered, that the grace and love of God to man may appear so much the greater the more widely this sacred communion is spread over the world.

Thanks be unto thee, O merciful JESU, thou eternal shepherd, that thou hast vouchsafed to refresh us, who are poor and in a state of banishment, with thy precious body and blood ; and to invite us to the receiving of these mysteries with the words even of thine own mouth, saying, " Come unto me, all ye that labour and are heavy laden, and I will refresh you."

CHAPTER II.

That the great Goodness and Love of God is Exhibited to Man in this Sacrament.

IN confidence of thy goodness and great mercy, O Lord, I draw near, as one sick to the Healer, as one hungry and thirsty to the Fountain of Life, needy to the King of heaven, a servant unto my Lord, a creature to my Creator, a desolate soul to my merciful Comforter.

But whence is this to me, that thou vouchsafest to come unto me? [1] What am I, that thou shouldst grant thine own self unto me?

How dare a sinner appear before thee? and how is it that thou dost vouchsafe to come unto a sinner?

Thou knowest thy servant, thou knowest that he hath in him no good thing for which thou shouldst grant him this favour.

I confess, therefore, mine own unworthiness, I acknowledge thy goodness, I praise thy tender mercy, and give thee thanks for this thy transcendent love.

For thou doest this for thine own sake, not for any merits of mine; to the end that thy goodness may be better known unto me, thy love more abundantly poured down, and thy gracious humility more eminently set forth.

Since, therefore, it is thy pleasure, and thou hast commanded that it should be so, this that seemeth to thee good pleaseth me also, and would that mine iniquity might be no hindrance!

2. O most sweet and most merciful JESU, how great reverence and thanksgiving, together with perpetual praise, is due unto thee for the receiving of thy sacred body and blood, whose preciousness no man is able to express!

But on what shall my thoughts dwell at this communion, in thus approaching unto my Lord,

[1] Luke i. [43].

whom I am not able duly to honour, and yet whom I cannot but desire devoutly to receive ?

3. What can I think on better, and more profitable, than utterly to humble myself before thee, and to exalt thine infinite goodness over me ?

I praise thee, my God, and will exalt thee for ever. I do despise myself, and cast myself down before thee, into the deep of mine own unworthiness.

Behold, thou art the Holy of Holies, and I the scum of sinners !

Behold, thou inclinest thyself unto me, and I am not worthy so much as to look up unto thee !

Behold, thou comest unto me ; it is thy will to be with me ; thou invitest me to thy banquet.

Thou art willing to give me heavenly food and bread of angels to eat,[1] which is indeed no other than thyself the living bread, which camest down from heaven, and givest life unto the world.

4. Behold, from whence doth this love proceed ! what gracious condescension shineth forth herein ! how great thanks and praises are due unto thee for these benefits !

O how great and profitable was thy counsel, when thou didst ordain it ! how sweet and pleasant the banquet, when thou gavest thyself to be our food !

O how admirable is this thy working, O Lord, how mighty is thy power, how unspeakable thy truth !

For thou didst speak the word and all things were made ;[2] and this was done which thou thyself commandedst.

5. A thing much to be admired, worthy of all

---

[1] Ps. lxxviii. [25] ; John vi. [33].   [2] Gen. i. ; Ps. cxlviii. [5].

faith, and surpassing man's understanding, that thou, my Lord God, true God and man, shouldst offer thyself wholly to us in a little bread and wine, and therein become our inexhaustible support.

Thou who art the Lord of the universe, and standest in need of none,[1] art pleased to dwell in us by means of this thy sacrament.

Do thou preserve my heart and body undefiled, that with a cheerful and pure conscience I may be able often to receive to my everlasting health those mysteries which thou didst specially ordain and institute for thine own honour, and for a never-ceasing memorial of thyself.

6. Rejoice, O my soul, and give thanks unto God, for so noble a gift and so precious a consolation, left unto thee in this vale of tears.

For as often as thou callest to mind this mystery, and receivest the body of Christ, so often dost thou go over the work of thy redemption, and art made partaker of all the merits of Christ.

For the love of Christ is never diminished, and the greatness of his propitiation is never exhausted.

Therefore thou oughtest to dispose thyself hereunto by a constant fresh renewing of thy mind, and to weigh with attentive consideration the great mystery of salvation.

So great, so new, and so joyful ought it to seem unto thee, when thou comest to these holy mysteries, as if on this same day Christ first descending into the womb of the virgin were become man, or hanging on the cross did this day suffer and die for the salvation of mankind.

[1] Ps. xvi. [2].

CHAPTER III.

That it is Profitable to Communicate often.

BEHOLD, O Lord, I come unto thee, that I may be comforted in thy gift, and be delighted in thy holy banquet, which thou, O God, hast of thy goodness prepared for the poor.[1]

Behold, in thee is all whatsoever I can or ought to desire ; and thou art my salvation and my redemption, my hope and my strength, my honour and glory.

Make, therefore, this day the soul of thy servant joyful ;[2] for unto thee, O Lord JESU, have I lifted up my soul.

I desire to receive thee now with devotion and reverence. I desire to bring thee into my house, that with Zaccheus I may be blessed by thee, and be numbered amongst the children of Abraham.

My soul thirsteth to receive thy body and blood, my heart longeth to be joined to thee.

2. Give thyself to me, and it sufficeth ; for beside thee there is no comfort.

Without thee I cannot be ; without thy visitation I cannot endure to live.

And therefore I must needs often draw near unto thee, and receive thee for the medicine of my soul ; lest haply I faint by the way, if I be deprived of this heavenly food.

For so, most merciful JESUS, thou once didst say, when preaching to the people, and curing divers

[1] Ps. lxviii. [10].   [2] Ps. lxxxvi. [4].

diseases, " I will not send them home fasting, lest they faint in the way." [1]

Deal thou therefore in like manner now with me, who hast vouchsafed to leave thyself in this sacrament for the comfort of the faithful.

For thou art the sweet refection of the soul ; and he that eateth thee worthily shall be partaker and heir of everlasting glory.

It is needful for me, who so often fall into error and sin, and so quickly wax dull and faint, that by frequent prayer and confession, and receiving of thy holy body and blood, I renew, cleanse, and inflame myself, lest haply, by long abstaining, I fall away from my holy purposes.

3. For the imaginations of man are prone unto evil from his youth,[2] and unless some divine remedy help him he quickly falleth away to worse things.

This holy communion, therefore, draweth men back from evil, and strengtheneth them in good.

For if I be now so often negligent and cold when I communicate, what would become of me if I received not this remedy, and sought not after so great a help ?

Although every day I be not fit nor well prepared, I will endeavour notwithstanding at due times to receive the divine mysteries, and to be partaker of so great a grace.

For this is the one chief consolation of faithful souls, so long as they are absent from thee in this mortal body, that being mindful of their God, they often receive their beloved with devout mind.

4. O the wonderful condescension of thy tender

---

[1] Matt. xv. [32] ; Mark viii. [3].　　[2] Gen. viii. [21].

mercy towards us, that thou, O Lord God, the creator and giver of life to all spirits, dost vouchsafe to come unto a poor soul, and with thy whole deity and humanity to appease the hunger thereof!

O happy minds and blessed souls who have the privilege of receiving thee, their Lord God, with devout affection, and in so receiving thee are permitted to be filled with spiritual joy!

O how great a Lord do they entertain! how beloved a guest do they harbour! how delightful a companion do they receive! how faithful a friend do they welcome! how lovely and noble a spouse do they embrace! even him who is to be loved above all things that are loved, and above all things that can be desired.

O thou the most sweet, most beloved, let heaven and earth, and all that adorns them, be silent in thy presence. For what praise and beauty soever they have, it is received from thy bounteous condescension, and shall never equal the grace and beauty of thy name, whose wisdom is infinite.[1]

CHAPTER IV.

That many Benefits are Bestowed upon those that Communicate Devoutly.

O LORD, my God, do thou prevent thy servant with the blessings of thy goodness,[2] that I may approach worthily and devoutly to thy glorious sacrament.

[1] Ps. cxlvii. [5].   [2] Ps. xxi. [3].

Stir up my heart unto thee, and deliver me from all dulness. Visit me with thy salvation,[1] that I may taste in spirit thy sweetness, which plentifully lieth hid in this sacrament as in a fountain.

Enlighten also mine eyes to behold so great a mystery, and strengthen me with undoubting faith to believe it.

For it is thy work, and no human power; thy sacred institution, not man's invention.

For of himself no man is able to comprehend and understand these things, which surpass the understanding even of angels.

What portion, then, of so high and sacred a mystery shall I, unworthy sinner, dust and ashes, be able to search out and comprehend?

2. O Lord, in the simplicity of my heart, with a good and firm faith, and at thy commandment, I draw near unto thee with hope and reverence; and do truly believe that thou art here present in this sacrament, both God and man.

Thy will is, that I should receive thee, and that I should unite myself unto thee in charity.

Wherefore I implore thy mercy, and do crave thy special grace, to the end I may wholly be dissolved and overflow with love unto thee, and never hereafter suffer any external consolation to enter in.

For this most high and precious sacrament is the health both of soul and body, the medicine for all spiritual languor; hereby my vices are cured, my passions bridled, my temptations overcome or at least weakened; greater grace is infused, virtue

[1] Ps. cxi. [4].

begun is increased, faith is confirmed, hope strengthened, and love inflamed and enlarged.

3. For thou hast bestowed, and still oftentimes dost bestow, many benefits in this sacrament upon thy beloved ones that communicate devoutly, O my God, the protector of my soul, the strengthener of human frailty, and the giver of all inward comfort.

Thou impartest unto them much comfort against sundry tribulations; and liftest them up from the depth of their own dejected state, to hope in thy protection; and dost inwardly refresh and enlighten them with new grace, so that they who at first and before communion felt themselves full of anxiety and heartlessness, afterwards, being refreshed with heavenly meat and drink, do find in themselves a change for the better.

And in such a way of dispensation thou dealest with thine elect, that they may truly acknowledge, and clearly prove, how great their own infirmity is, and what goodness and grace they obtain from thee.

For they of themselves are cold, dull, and undevout; but by thee they are made fervent, cheerful, and full of devotion.

For who is there that, approaching humbly unto the fountain of sweetness, doth not carry away from thence at least some little sweetness?

Or who, standing by a great fire, receiveth not some small heat thereby?

And thou art a fountain always full and overflowing, a fire ever burning and never decaying.[1]

4. Wherefore, if I am not permitted to draw

[1] Isa. xii. [3]; Lev. vi. [13].

out of the full fountain itself, nor to drink my fill, I will notwithstanding set my lips to the mouth of this heavenly conduit, that I may receive from thence at least some small drop to refresh my thirst, that so I may not be wholly dried up.

And though I cannot as yet be altogether heavenly, nor so full of love as the cherubim and seraphim, yet notwithstanding I will endeavour to apply myself earnestly to devotion, and prepare my heart to obtain if it be but some small spark of divine fire, by the humble receiving of this life-giving sacrament.

And whatsoever is hereunto wanting in me, O merciful JESU, most holy Saviour, do thou bountifully and graciously supply for me, thou who hast vouchsafed to call us all unto thee, saying, " Come unto me, all ye that labour and are heavy laden, and I will refresh you." [1]

5. I indeed labour in the sweat of my brows,[2] I am vexed with grief of heart, I am burdened with sins, I am troubled with temptations, I am entangled and oppressed with many evil passions ; and there is none to help me, none to deliver and save me, but thou, O Lord God my Saviour, to whom I commit myself and all that is mine, that thou mayest keep watch over me, and bring me safe to life everlasting.

Receive me for the honour and glory of thy name, thou who hast prepared thy body and blood to be my meat and drink.

Grant, O Lord God, my Saviour, that by frequenting the celebration of thy mysteries the zeal of my devotion may grow and increase.

[1] Matt. xi. [28].   [2] Gen. iii. [19].

CHAPTER V.

Of the Dignity of this Sacrament, and of the Ministerial Function.

IF thou hadst the purity of an angel,[1] and the sanctity of St. John Baptist, thou wouldst not be worthy to receive or to administer this sacrament.

For it is not within the compass of the deserts of men that man should consecrate and administer this sacrament of Christ, and receive for food the bread of angels.[2]

Great is this mystery; and great is the dignity of those to whom is granted that which is not permitted to angels.

For only priests rightly ordained in the church have power to celebrate this sacrament, and to consecrate the body of Christ.

The priest is indeed the minister of God, using the word of God, by God's command and appointment: but God is there the principal author and invisible worker; to whom is subject all that he shall please, and whom everything that he commandeth doth obey.[3]

2. Thou oughtest therefore more to believe God Almighty in this most excellent sacrament than thine own sense or any visible sign.

And therefore thou art to approach this holy work with fear and reverence.

Consider attentively with thyself,[4] and see what

---

[1] Matt. xviii. [10]. [2] Ps. lxxviii. [25].
[3] Gen. i.; Ps. xlix. [7]; Rom. ix. [20]. [4] 1 Tim. iv. [16].

that is whereof the ministry is delivered unto thee by the laying on of the bishop's hand.

Behold, thou art made a priest, and consecrated to celebrate the Lord's sacrament ; take heed now that thou offer this sacrifice to God faithfully and devoutly, and at fit opportunities, and conduct thyself so as thou mayest be without reproof.

Thou hast not lightened thy burden, but art now bound with a straiter band of discipline, and art obliged to a more perfect degree of sanctity.

A priest ought to be adorned with all graces, and to give example of good life to others.

His life and conversation [1] should not be in the common ways of mankind, but with the angels in heaven, or with perfect men on earth.

3. A priest clad in sacred garments is Christ's deputy, that with all supplication and humility he may beseech God for himself and for the whole people.[2]

Neither ought he to cease from prayer and holy oblation till he prevail to obtain grace and mercy.

When a priest doth celebrate the holy eucharist, he honoureth God, he rejoiceth the angels, he edifieth the church, he helpeth the living, he maketh mention of the departed, and maketh himself partaker of all good things.

[1] Phil. iii. [20].   [2] Heb. v. [3].

CHAPTER VI.

An Inquiry concerning Spiritual Exercise before Communion.

WHEN I weigh thy worthiness, O Lord, and mine own vileness, I tremble exceedingly, and am confounded within myself.

For if I come not unto thee, I fly from life ; and if I unworthily intrude myself, I incur thy displeasure.

What therefore shall I do, O my God, my helper and my counsellor in all necessity ?

2. Teach thou me the right way, appoint me some brief exercise suitable to this holy communion.

For it is good for me to know how I should reverently and religiously prepare my heart for thee, for the profitable receiving of this sacrament of thine, or for the celebrating of so great and divine a sacrifice.

CHAPTER VII.

Of Thoroughly Searching our own Conscience, and of Holy Purposes of Amendment.

ABOVE all things, God's priest ought to come to celebrate and to receive this sacrament with very great humility of heart, and with reverential supplication, with a full faith and a dutiful regard for God's honour.

Examine diligently thy conscience, and to the

9

utmost of thy power purify and cleanse it with true contrition and humble confession ; so as there may be nothing in thee that may be burdensome unto thee, or that may breed in thee remorse of conscience, and hinder thy free access to the throne of grace.

Be grieved at the recollection of all thy sins in general, and in particular bewail and lament thy daily transgressions.

And if thou hast time, confess unto God in the secret of thine heart all the miserable evils of thy disordered passions.

2. Lament thou and grieve that thou art yet so carnal and worldly, so unmortified in thy passions, so full of the motions of concupiscence :

So unwatchful over thy outward senses, so often entangled with many vain fancies :

So much inclined to outward things, so negligent in things inward and spiritual :

So prone to laughter and unbridled mirth, so indisposed to tears and compunction :

So prompt to ease and the pleasures of the flesh, so dull to strictness of life and zeal :

So curious to hear news and to see beautiful sights, so slack to embrace what is humble and low :

So covetous of abundance, so niggardly in giving, so fast in keeping :

So inconsiderate in speech, so reluctant to keep silence :

So uncomposed in manners, so fretful in action :

So eager about food, so deaf to the word of God :

In such a hurry to rest, so slow to labour :

So wakeful in vain conversation, so drowsy at sacred services :

So hasty to arrive at the end thereof, so inclined to be wandering and inattentive :

So negligent in the prayers, so lukewarm in celebrating the holy eucharist, so dry and heartless in receiving it :

So quickly distracted, so seldom wholly gathered into thyself :

So suddenly moved to anger, so apt to take displeasure against another :

So ready to judge, so severe to reprove :

So joyful in prosperity, so weak in adversity :

So often making good resolutions, and yet bringing them at last to so poor effect.

3. These and other thy defects being confessed and bewailed with sorrow and great displeasure at thine own infirmity, make thou a firm resolution always to be amending thy life, and to be endeavouring always after a further progress in holiness.

Then with full resignation and with thy whole will, do thou, to the honour of my name, offer up thyself a perpetual whole burnt offering on the altar of thy heart, faithfully committing thy body and soul unto me.

And then thou mayest be accounted worthy to draw near to celebrate this eucharistical sacrifice unto God, and to receive profitably the sacrament of my body and blood.

4. For man hath no oblation more worthy, nor any means greater for the destroying of sin, than to offer himself unto God purely and wholly in the holy communion of the body and blood of Christ.

And when a man shall have done what lieth in him, and shall be truly penitent, how often soever he shall come to me for pardon and grace, " As I live," saith the Lord, " who will not the death of a sinner, but rather that he be converted and live,[1] I will not remember his sins any more, but they shall all be forgiven him."

CHAPTER VIII.

Of the Oblation of Christ on the Cross, and of Resignation of Ourselves.

OF my own will did I offer up myself unto God the Father for thy sins.[2] My hands were stretched forth on the cross, and my body laid bare, so that nothing remained in me that was not wholly turned into a sacrifice for the appeasing of the divine Majesty.

In like manner oughtest thou also to offer thyself willingly unto me in the holy communion, as a pure and sacred oblation, with all thy strength and affections, and to the utmost of thine inward faculties.

What do I require of thee more than that thou study to resign thyself entirely unto me ?

Whatsoever thou givest besides thyself is of no value in my sight, for I seek not thy gifts, but thee.[3]

2. As it would not suffice thee to have all things whatsoever, without me ; so neither can it please me, whatsoever thou givest, if thou give not thyself.

---

[1] Ezek. xviii. [22, 23].   [2] Isa. liii. [5]; Heb. ix. [28].
[3] Prov. xxiii. [26].

Offer up thyself unto me, and give thyself wholly for God, and thine offering shall be acceptable.

Behold, I offered up myself wholly unto my Father for thee, and gave my whole body and blood for thy food, that I might be wholly thine, and that thou mightest continue mine to the end.

But if thou abidest in thyself, and dost not offer thyself up freely unto my will, thine oblation is not entire, neither will there be perfect union between us.

Therefore a free offering of thyself into the hands of God ought to go before all thine actions, if thou desire to obtain liberty and grace.

For this cause so few become inwardly free and enlightened, because they are loath wholly to deny themselves.

My sentence standeth sure, " Unless a man forsake all, he cannot be my disciple." [1] If thou therefore desire to be my disciple, offer up thyself unto me with thy whole heart.

CHAPTER IX.

That we ought to offer up Ourselves and all that is ours unto God, and to Pray for All.

THINE, O Lord, are all things that are in heaven, and that are in earth.[2]

I desire to offer up myself unto thee, as a free oblation, and to continue thine for ever.

[1] Luke xiv. [33].   [2] Ps. xxiv. [1].

O Lord, in the simplicity of my heart, I offer myself unto thee this day, in humble submission, for a sacrifice of perpetual praise, and to be thy servant for ever.

Receive thou me, with this holy oblation of thy precious body; which offering I make to thee this day in the presence of angels invisibly attending; and may this be for my good and the good of all thy people.

2. I offer unto thee, O Lord, all my sins and offences, which I have committed before thee, from the day wherein I first could sin to this hour. I offer them upon thy merciful altar, that thou mayest consume and burn them all with the fire of thy love; that thou mayest wash out all the stains of my sins. Cleanse my conscience from all offences, and restore to me again thy grace, which I have lost by sin, forgiving me all my offences, and receiving me mercifully to the kiss of peace.

3. What can I do for my sins,[1] but humbly confess and bewail them, and unceasingly entreat thy favour and propitiation?

I beseech thee, hear me graciously, when I stand before thee my God.

All my sins are very displeasing unto me. I will never commit them any more; but I grieve, and will grieve for them as long as I live, and am purposed to repent, and, according to the utmost of my power, to make restitution.

Forgive me, O God, forgive me my sins for the sake of thy holy name; save thou my soul, which thou hast redeemed with thy most precious blood.

[1] Ps. xxxii. [5].

Of Offering up to God all that is Ours.

Behold, I commit myself unto thy mercy, I re[...]
myself into thy hands.

Deal with me according to thy goodness, not
according to my wickedness and iniquity.

4. I offer up also unto thee all whatsoever is good
in me, although it be very small and imperfect,
that thou mayest amend and sanctify it. Make
it grateful and acceptable unto thee, and always
perfect it more and more ; and bring me also, who
am a slothful and unprofitable creature, to a good
and blessed end.

5. I offer up also unto thee all the pious desires
of devout persons, the necessities of parents, friends,
brethren, sisters, and of all those that are dear unto
me, and that have done good either to myself or
to others for thy love.

Also all that have desired of me to pray for them
and theirs.

Grant that all may receive the help of thy grace,
the aid of thy consolation, protection from dangers,
deliverance from pain ; that they, being freed
from all evils, may with joy return abundant thanks-
givings unto thee.

6. I offer up also unto thee my prayers and inter-
cessions for those especially who have in anything
wronged, grieved, or slandered me, or have done
me any damage or displeasure.

I pray for all those also whom I have at any time
vexed, troubled, grieved, and scandalized by words
or deeds, knowingly or in ignorance ; that it may
please thee to forgive us all our sins and offences,
one against another.

Take away from our hearts, O Lord, all suspicious-

ness, indignation, wrath, and contention, and whatsoever may hurt charity and lessen brotherly love.

Have mercy, O Lord, have mercy on those that
crave thy mercy, give grace unto them that stand
in need thereof, and make us such as that we may
be counted worthy to enjoy thy grace and go forward to life eternal.. *Amen.*

CHAPTER X.

That the Holy Communion is not Lightly to be Forborne.

THOU oughtest often to have recourse to the fountain of grace and of divine mercy, to the fountain
of goodness and of all purity, that thou mayest be
healed of thy sins and passions, and be made more
strong and vigilant against all the temptations and
deceits of the devil.

The enemy, knowing what exceeding great profit
and restoring power cometh by the holy communion,
endeavoureth by all means and occasions to withdraw and hinder faithful and devout persons from
partaking therein.

2. Thus it is that some persons, when they are
preparing to fit themselves for holy communion,
suffer from the suggestions of Satan worse than
before.

That wicked spirit himself (as it is written in Job)
cometh amongst the sons of God [1] to trouble them

[1] Job i. [6].

according to his accustomed malice, or to render them over fearful and perplexed, that so he may diminish their affections, or by direct assaults take away their faith, to the end he may prevail on them, if possible, either altogether to forbear communicating, or at least to come with lukewarmness.

But there is no heed at all to be taken of these his crafty and fanciful suggestions, be they ever so filthy and hideous, but all such vain imaginations are to be turned back upon his own head.

Thou must despise him and laugh him to scorn, nor dare to omit the holy communion on account of his assaults, or for the troubles which he raiseth within thee.

3. Oftentimes, also, a too great solicitude for the obtaining a certain height of devotion, and a kind of anxiety about the confession of sins, hindereth thee.

Follow herein the counsel of the wise,[1] and lay aside all anxiety and scrupulousness ; for it hindereth the grace of God, and overthroweth the devotion of the mind.

Do not omit the holy communion for every small vexation and trouble, but rather proceed at once to confess thy sins, and cheerfully forgive others whatever offences they have done against thee.

And if thou hast offended any, humbly crave pardon, and God will readily forgive thee.[2]

4. What availeth it to delay long the confession of thy sins, or to defer the holy communion ?

Make thyself thoroughly clean as soon as possible. Spit out the poison with all speed, make haste to

[1] Prov. xiii.   [2] Matt. vi. [14].

apply this sovereign remedy, and thou shalt find it to be better with thee than if thou long defer it.

If thou omit it to-day for one cause, perhaps to-morrow another of greater force may occur to thee ; and so thou mayest be hindered a long time from communion, and grow more and more unfit.

As quickly as ever thou canst, shake off from thyself all present heaviness and sloth. For it is of no use to continue long in disquietness, or to be going on long with a disturbed conscience, and so for every-day impediments to separate thyself from this divine service.

Yea, it is very hurtful to defer the communion long, for this usually brings on heavy spiritual drowsiness.

Alas, some lukewarm undisciplined persons do willingly delay confessing their sins, and defer the holy communion, lest they should be engaged to keep a stricter watch over themselves !

5. Oh how poor and mean is their love, how weak their devotion, who so easily put off the holy communion !

How happy is he, and how acceptable to God, who so ordereth his life, and in such purity keepeth his conscience, that he is prepared and well-disposed to communicate even every day, if it were in his power, and if it might be done without being seen of men.

If a person do sometimes abstain out of humility, or by reason of some lawful cause preventing him, he is to be commended so far as it ariseth from a feeling of reverence.

But if a spiritual drowsiness have crept over him, he must bestir himself, and do what lieth in him ;

and the Lord will assist his desire, for the good-will he hath thereto, which is what God doth chiefly respect.

6. But when any lawful hindrance doth happen, he will yet always have a good will, and a pious intention to communicate; and so shall he not lose the fruit of this sacrament.

For any devout person may every day and every hour profitably and without let draw near to Christ in spiritual communion.

And yet on certain days, and at times appointed, he ought to receive sacramentally, with affectionate reverence, the body and blood of his Redeemer, and rather seek the honour and glory of God than his own comfort.[1]

For he communicateth mystically, and is invisibly refreshed, as often as he devoutly calleth to mind the mystery of the incarnation and the passion of Christ, and is inflamed with the love of him.

7. He that prepareth not himself, except only when a festival draweth near, or when custom compelleth him thereunto, shall too often be unprepared.

Blessed is he that offereth up himself as a whole burnt offering to the Lord, as often as he doth administer or receive the holy communion.

Be not too slow nor yet hurried in celebrating, but keep the accustomed manner of those with whom thou livest.

Thou oughtest not to be tedious and troublesome to others, but to observe the received custom, according to the appointment of our fathers; and rather to yield thyself up to the edification of others than to thine own devotion or feelings.

[1] I Cor. xi.

CHAPTER XI.

That the Body and Blood of Christ and the Holy Scrip-
tures are most Necessary unto a Faithful Soul.

O BLESSED Lord JESUS, how great is the happiness
of a devout soul that feasteth with thee in thy banquet ; where there is set no other food to be eaten
but thyself, the only Beloved, and most to be desired
above all the desires of the heart !

And verily it would be a sweet thing unto me in
thy presence to pour out tears from the very bottom
of my heart, and with grateful Magdalene to wash
thy feet with tears.[1]

But where now is that devotion ? where that
plentiful effusion of holy tears ?

Surely in the sight of thee and thy holy angels my
whole heart ought to be inflamed, and even to weep
for joy.

For in this sacrament I have thee truly present,
though hidden under another representation.

2. For to behold thee in thine own divine brightness mine eyes would not be able to endure, nor could
even the whole world stand in the splendour of the
glory of thy majesty.

Herein then dost thou have regard to my weakness,
that thou dost veil thyself under this outward sacramental sign.

Him I do really possess and adore whom the angels
adore in heaven : but I, for the present and in the
meantime, by faith ; they, by sight, and without a
veil.

[1] Luke vii. [38].

I ought to be content with the light of true faith,
and to walk therein, until the day of everlasting
brightness dawn and the shadows of figures pass
away.

But when that which is perfect is come, the use
of sacraments shall cease; [1] because the blessed, in
their heavenly glory, need not any sacramental
remedy.

For they rejoice without end in the presence of
God, beholding his glory face to face; and being
transformed from glory to glory into his image, they
taste the WORD of God made flesh, as he was from
the beginning, and as he abideth for ever.

3. Whilst I am mindful of these wonderful things,
it becometh tedious unto me, even all spiritual comfort whatsoever; because as long as I behold not my
Lord openly in his own glory, I make no account
at all of whatsoever I see or hear in this world.

Thou art witness unto me, O God, that nothing
can comfort me, no creature can give me rest, but
thou only, my God, whom I long to contemplate
everlastingly.

But this is not possible so long as I linger in this
mortality.

Therefore I must frame myself to much patience,
and submit myself to thee in all my desires.

For even thy saints, O Lord, who now rejoice with
thee in the kingdom of heaven, whilst they lived,
waited in faith and in great patience for the coming
of thy glory.[2] What they believed, I believe also;
what they hoped for, I hope for; whither they are
arrived, I trust I shall arrive by thy grace.

[1] i Cor. xiii. [10].   [2] Heb. x. [35, 36], xi.

In the meantime I will walk in faith, strengthened by the examples of the saints.

I have also holy books for my comfort and for the glass of my life ; and above all these, thy most holy body and blood for a remedy and refuge.

4. For I perceive two things to be very particularly necessary for me in this life, without which it would be unsupportable unto me.

Whilst I am detained in the prison of this body, I acknowledge myself to stand in need of two things— namely, food and light.

Unto me then, thus weak and helpless, thou hast given thy sacred body, for the refreshment both of my soul and body ; [1] and thy word thou hast set as a light unto my feet. [2]

Without these two I should not be able to live ; for the word of God is the light of my soul, and thy sacrament the bread of life.

These also may be called the two tables, set on the one side and on the other, in the treasury and jewel-house of the holy church. [3]

One table is that of the sacred altar, having the holy bread ; that is, the precious body of Christ. The other is that of the divine law, containing holy doctrine, teaching men the right faith, and steadily conducting them forward even to that within the veil, where is the holy of holies.

Thanks be unto thee, O Lord JESU, thou Light of everlasting Light, for that table of holy doctrine which thou hast prepared for us by thy servants the prophets and apostles and other teachers.

---

[1] John vi. [51].   [2] Ps. cxix. [105].
[3] Ps. xxiii. [5] ; Heb. ix. [2], xiii. [10].

5. Thanks be unto thee, O thou Creator and Redeemer of mankind, who, to manifest thy love to the whole world, hast prepared a great supper,[1] wherein thou hast set before us to be eaten, not the typical lamb, but thine own most sacred body and blood,[2] rejoicing all the faithful with this holy banquet, and replenishing them to the full with the cup of salvation,[3] in which are all the delights of paradise; and the holy angels do feast with us, but yet with a more happy sweetness.

6. Oh, how great and honourable is the office of God's priests, to whom it is given with sacred words to consecrate this sacrament of the LORD of glory; with their lips to bless, with their hands to hold, with their own mouth to receive, and also to administer to others!

Oh, how clean ought those hands to be, how pure that mouth, how holy that body, how unspotted that heart, where the Author of purity so often entereth!

Nothing but what is holy, no word but what is good and profitable, ought to proceed from the mouth of him who so often receiveth this sacrament of Christ.

7. Simple and chaste ought to be the eyes that are wont to behold the body of Christ; the hands should be pure and lifted up to heaven that are used to touch these emblems of the Creator of heaven and earth.

Unto the priests especially it is said in the law, " Be ye holy, for that I the LORD your God am holy." [4]

---

[1] Luke xiv. [16].
[2] John vi. [53–56].
[3] Ps. xxiii. [5]; Wisd. xvi. [20, 21].
[4] Lev. xix. [2], xx. [26].

8. O Almighty God, do thou assist us with thy grace, that we who have undertaken the office of the priesthood may be able to serve thee worthily and devoutly, in all purity, and with a good conscience.

And if we live not in so great innocency as we ought to do, grant to us at the least worthily to lament the sins which we have committed ; and in the spirit of humility, and with the full purpose of a good will, to serve thee more earnestly for the time to come.

CHAPTER XII.

That He who is about to Communicate with Christ ought to Prepare Himself with great Diligence.

I AM the lover of purity and the giver of all sanctity.

I seek a pure heart, and there is the place of my rest.[1]

Make ready for me a large upper room furnished,[2] and I will keep the passover at thy house with my disciples.

If thou wilt have me come unto thee, and remain with thee, purge out the old leaven,[3] and make clean the habitation of thy heart.

Shut out the whole world,[4] and all the throng of sins ; sit thou as it were a sparrow alone upon the house-top, and think over thy transgressions in the bitterness of thy soul.

[1] Ps. xxiv. [4] ; Matt. v. [8].
[2] Mark xiv. [14, 15] ; Luke xxii. [11, 12].
[3] I Cor. v. [7].   [4] Ex. xxiv. [18].

For every one that loveth will prepare the best and fairest place for his beloved ; for herein is known the affection of him that entertaineth his beloved.

2. Know thou, notwithstanding, that the merit of no action of thine is able to make this preparation sufficient, although thou shouldst prepare thyself a whole year together, and have nothing else in thy mind.

But it is out of my mere grace and favour that thou art permitted to come to my table. As if a beggar were invited to a rich man's dinner, and he hath no other return to make to him for his benefits but to humble himself and give him thanks.

Do what lieth in thee, and do it diligently ; not for custom, not for necessity, but with fear and reverence and affection receive the body and blood of thy beloved Saviour, when he vouchsafeth to come unto thee.

I am he that have called thee, I have commanded it to be done, I will supply what is wanting in thee ; come thou and receive me.

3. When I bestow on thee the grace of devotion, give thanks to thy God ; not because thou art worthy, but because I have had mercy on thee.

If thou have it not, but rather dost feel thyself dry, be instant in prayer, sigh and knock, and give not over until thou have received some crumb or drop of saving grace.

Thou hast need of me ; I have no need of thee.

Neither comest thou to sanctify me ; but I come to sanctify and make thee holy.

Thou comest that thou mayest be sanctified by me, and united unto me, that thou mayest receive new grace, and be stirred up anew to amendment of life.

Neglect not this grace, but prepare thy heart with all diligence, and receive thy beloved into thy soul.

4. But thou oughtest not only to prepare thyself to devotion before communion, but carefully also to preserve thyself therein, after thou hast received this sacrament.

Nor is the careful guard of thyself afterwards less required than devout preparation before.

For a good guard afterwards is the best preparation again for the obtaining of greater grace.

For if a person gives himself up at once too much to outward consolations, he is rendered thereby greatly indisposed to devotion.

Beware of much talk,[1] remain in some secret place, and enjoy thy God ; for thou hast him whom all the world cannot take from thee.

I am he to whom thou oughtest wholly to give up thyself, that so thou mayest now live the rest of thy time, not in thyself, but in me, and be free from all anxious care.

CHAPTER XIII.

That the Devout Soul ought with the whole Heart to Seek Union with Christ in this Sacrament.

How shall I obtain this favour, O Lord, to find thee alone and by thyself, to open unto thee my whole

[1] Prov. x. [19].

heart, and to enjoy thee even as my soul desireth?
so that henceforth none may look upon me, nor any
creature move me, nor have regard to me : but that
thou alone mayest speak unto me, and I to thee, as
the beloved is wont to speak to his beloved, and a
friend to banquet with his friend.[1]

This I beg, this I long for, that I may be wholly
united unto thee, and may withdraw my heart from
all created things, and may learn more and more
by means of this sacred communion, and the often
celebrating thereof, to relish things heavenly and
eternal.

Ah, Lord God, when shall I be wholly united to
thee, and absorbed by thee, and become altogether
forgetful of myself ?

" Thou in me, and I in thee ; "[2] so also grant that
we may both continue together in one.

2. Verily, thou art my beloved, the choicest
amongst thousands,[3] in whom my soul is well
pleased to dwell all the days of her life.

Verily, thou art my peacemaker, in whom is
highest peace and true rest, out of whom is labour
and sorrow and infinite misery.

Verily, thou art a God that hidest thyself,[4] and
thy counsel is not with the wicked, but thy speech
is with the humble and simple of heart.[5]

O how sweet is thy spirit, O Lord, who, to the end
thou mightest show forth thy sweetness toward thy
children, dost vouchsafe to feed them with the
bread which is full of all sweetness, even that which
cometh down from heaven.[6]

[1] Ex. xxxiii. [11]; Cant. viii. [2]. [2] John xv. [4]. [3] Cant. v. [10].
[4] Isa. xlv. [15]. [5] Prov. iii. [34]. [6] Wisd. xvi. [20, 21].

Surely there is no other nation so great,[1] that hath God so nigh unto them, as thou our God art present to all thy faithful ones, unto whom, for their daily comfort and for the raising up of their hearts to heaven, thou bestowest thyself.

3. For what other nation is there of such high renown as the Christian people?

Or what creature under heaven is there so beloved as the devout soul, into which God himself entereth, to nourish it with himself!

O unspeakable grace! O admirable condescension! O immeasurable love specially bestowed on man!

But what return shall I make to the Lord for this grace,[2] for charity so unparalleled?

There is nothing else that I am able to present more acceptable than to offer my heart wholly to my God, and to unite it most inwardly unto him.

Then shall all my inward parts rejoice, when my soul shall be perfectly united unto God.

Then will he say unto me, " If thou art willing to be with me, I am willing to be with thee."

And I will answer him, " Vouchsafe, O Lord, to remain with me, for I will gladly be with thee.

" This is my whole desire, that my heart be united unto thee."

[1] Deut. iv. [7]. [2] Ps. cxvi. [12].

CHAPTER XIV.

*Of the Fervent Desire of some Devout Persons to
Receive the Body and Blood of Christ.*

O HOW great is the abundance of thy goodness, O
Lord, which thou hast laid up for them that fear
thee ! [1]

When I call to mind some devout persons, who
approach to this thy sacrament, O Lord, with the
greatest devotion and affection, I am oftentimes
confounded, and blush within myself, that I come
with such lukewarmness, yea, coldness, to thine
altar and the table of sacred communion.

I grieve that I remain so dry, and without hearty
affection ; that I am not wholly inflamed in thy
presence, O my God, and not so earnestly drawn
and affected as many devout persons have been.

For there have been some who, out of a vehement
desire of the holy communion and strong affection of
heart, could not restrain themselves from weeping.
And these, with desire, both of soul and body, earnestly longed after thee, O God, the fountain of life ;
not being otherwise able to allay or satisfy their
hunger, but by receiving thy body and blood with
all delight and spiritual eagerness.

2. O the truly ardent faith of such ! a clear argu-
ment of thy sacred presence.

For they truly know their Lord in the breaking
of bread,[2] whose heart within them so vehemently
burneth whilst thou, O blessed JESU, dost walk and
converse with them.

[1] Ps. xxxi. [19].   [2] Luke xxiv. [32, 35].

Such affection and devotion as this, love and fervency so vehement, are too often far from me.

Be thou favourable unto me, O merciful JESU, sweet and gracious Lord, and grant to me, thy poor needy creature, sometimes at least in this holy communion, to feel if it be but a small portion of thy hearty love, that my faith may become more strong, my hope in thy goodness may be increased, and that charity once perfectly kindled within me after the testing of this heavenly manna, may never decay.

3. But thy mercy is able to grant me the grace which I long for, and in the day when it shall please thee to visit me most mercifully with the spirit of fervour.

For although I burn not with such vehement desire as those who are so specially devoted to thee, yet notwithstanding, by thy grace, I long for this great and burning desire, praying from the heart that I may participate with all such thy fervent lovers, and be numbered among them in their holy company.

CHAPTER XV.

That the Grace of Devotion is Obtained by Humility and Denial of Ourselves.

THOU oughtest to seek the grace of devotion instantly, to ask it earnestly, to wait for it with patience and confidence, to receive it with thankfulness, to keep it humbly, to work with it diligently, and to commit the term and manner of this heavenly visitation to God, until it shall please him to come unto thee.

Thou oughtest especially to humble thyself, when thou feelest inwardly little or no devotion ; and yet not to be too much dejected, nor to grieve inordinately.

God often giveth in one short moment that which he for a long time hath denied ; he giveth sometimes in the end that which in the beginning of thy prayer he deferred to grant.

2. If grace were always presently given, and were ever at hand with a wish, weak man could not well bear it.

Therefore the grace of devotion is to be waited for with good hope and humble patience.

Nevertheless, do thou impute it to thyself, and to thine own sins, when this grace is not given thee, or when it is secretly taken away.

It is sometimes but a small matter that hindereth and hideth grace from us ; at least if anything can be called small, and not rather a weighty matter, which hindereth so great a good.

But if thou remove this, be it great or small, and perfectly overcome it, thou shalt have thy desire.

3. For immediately, as soon as thou givest thyself to God from thy whole heart, and seekest neither this nor that, according to thine own pleasure or will, but settlest thyself wholly in him, thou shalt find thyself united to him, and at peace ; for nothing can afford so sweet a relish, nothing can be so delightful, as the good pleasure of the divine will.

Whosoever, therefore, with a single heart, lifteth up his intention to God, and keepeth himself clear of all inordinate love or dislike of any created thing, he shall be the most fit to receive grace, and meet for the gift of true devotion.

For the Lord bestoweth his blessings there, where he findeth the vessels empty.

And the more perfectly a man forsaketh these low things, and the more he dieth to himself by contempt of himself, the more speedily shall grace come, and shall enter in the more plentifully, and shall lift up the free heart higher.

4. Then shall he see, and flow together, and wonder, and his heart shall be enlarged [1] within him ; because the hand of the Lord is with him, and he hath put himself wholly into his hand, even for ever and ever.

Behold, thus shall the man be blessed who seeketh God with his whole heart, and receiveth not his soul in vain.

This man, in receiving the holy eucharist, obtaineth the great favour of divine union ; for that he looketh not to his own devotion and comfort, but above all devotion and comfort to the honour and glory of God.

CHAPTER XVI.

That we ought to Lay Open our Necessities to Christ, and to Crave his Grace.

O THOU most sweet and loving Lord, whom I now desire to receive with all devotion, thou knowest my

Isa. lx. [5].

infirmities, and the necessities which I endure ; in how many sins and evils I am involved ; how often I am weighed down, tempted, disturbed, and defiled.

Unto thee I come for remedy, I entreat of thee consolation and support.

I speak to thee who knowest all things, to whom all my inward thoughts are open, and who alone canst perfectly comfort and help me.

Thou knowest what good things I stand in most need of, and how poor I am in all virtue.

2. Behold, I stand before thee poor and naked, calling for grace, and imploring mercy.

Refresh thy hungry supplicant, inflame my coldness with the fire of thy love, enlighten my blindness with the brightness of thy presence.

Do thou for me turn all earthly things into bitterness, all things grievous and contrary into patience, all low and created things into contempt and oblivion.

Lift up my heart to thee in heaven, and do not send me away to wander over the earth.

Be thou alone sweet unto me from henceforth for evermore ; for thou alone art my meat and drink, my love and my joy, my sweetness and all my good.

3. O that with thy presence thou wouldst wholly inflame, burn, and conform me unto thyself; that I might be made one spirit with thee,[1] by the grace of inward union, and by the meltings of ardent love !

Suffer me not to go away from thee hungry and dry, but deal mercifully with me, as oftentimes thou hast dealt wonderfully with thy saints.

[1] 1 Cor. vi. [17].

What marvel is it if I should be wholly inflamed by thee, and from myself fail and come to nothing; since thou art a fire alway burning and never decaying, a love purifying the heart and enlightening the understanding.

CHAPTER XVII.

Of Fervent Love, and Vehement Desire to Receive Christ.

WITH deep devotion and ardent love, with all affection and fervour of heart, I desire to receive thee, O Lord, as many saints and devout persons have desired thee, when they were partakers of thy holy communion; who in holiness of life were to thee most pleasing, and who in devotion also were most fervent.

O my God, my everlasting love, my whole good, my never-ending happiness, I desire to receive thee with the most earnest affection and the most worthy awe and reverence that any of the saints ever had or could feel toward thee.

2. And although I be unworthy to entertain all those feelings of devotion, nevertheless I offer unto thee the whole affection of my heart, as if I alone had all these most ardent longings.

Yea, and all that a dutiful mind can conceive and desire do I, with the deepest reverence and most inward affection, offer and present unto thee.

I desire to reserve nothing to myself, but freely

and most cheerfully to sacrifice unto thee myself
and all that is mine.

O Lord my God, my Creator and my Redeemer,
I do desire to receive thee this day with such affection, reverence, praise, and honour, with such gratitude, worthiness, and love, with such faith, hope, and
purity, as thy most holy mother, the glorious virgin
Mary, received and desired thee, when, to the angel
who declared unto her glad tidings of the mystery
of the incarnation, she humbly and devoutly an-
swered, " Behold the handmaid of the Lord; let it
be done unto me according to thy word." [1]

3. And as thy blessed forerunner, the most excellent among the saints, John Baptist, rejoicing in
thy presence, leaped for joy of the Holy Ghost whilst
he was yet shut up in his mother's womb; [2] and
afterwards seeing JESUS walking among men,
humbled himself very greatly, and said with devout
affection, " The friend of the bridegroom that
standeth and heareth him, rejoiceth greatly because
of the voice of the bridegroom;" [3] in like manner I
also wish to be inflamed with great and holy desires,
and to offer myself up to thee from my whole heart.

Wherefore also I offer and present unto thee the
triumphant joys, the fervent affections, the ecstasies,
the supernatural illuminations and celestial visions
of all devout hearts, with all the virtues and praises
ever celebrated by all creatures in heaven, and in
earth, for myself, and for all such as are commended
to me in prayer; that by all thou mayest worthily
be praised and for ever glorified.

4. Receive, O Lord my God, my wishes and desires

[1] Luke i. [38].   [2] Luke i. [44].   [3] John iii. [29].

of giving thee infinite praise, and blessing that hath no bounds ; which, according to the measure of thine ineffable greatness, are most justly due unto thee.

These praises I render unto thee, and long to render them every day and every moment. And with all entreaty and affectionateness I do invite and beseech all heavenly spirits, and all thy faithful servants, to render with me thanks and praises unto thee.

5. Let all people, nations, and languages praise thee,[1] and magnify thy holy and precious name with highest joy and ardent devotion.

And let all who reverently and devoutly celebrate thy most high sacrament, and receive it with full faith, be accounted worthy to find grace and mercy at thy hands, and pray with humble supplication in behalf of me a sinner.

And when they shall have attained to their desired devotion, and joyful union with thee, and shall have departed from thy holy heavenly table, well comforted and marvellously refreshed, O let them vouchsafe to remember my poor soul.

CHAPTER XVIII.

That a Man should not be a Curious Searcher into the Holy Sacrament, but an Humble Follower of Christ, Submitting his Sense to Divine Faith.

THOU oughtest to beware of curious and unprofitable searching into this most profound sacrament, if thou wilt not be plunged into the depths of doubt.

[1] Ps. cxvii.

He that is a searcher of my majesty shall be over-powered by its glory. God is able to work more than man can understand.

A dutiful and humble inquiry after the truth is allowable, provided we be always ready to be taught, and study to walk in the sound doctrine of the church.

2. It is a blessed simplicity when a man leaves the difficult ways of questions and disputings, and goes forward in the plain and firm path of God's commandments.

Many have lost devotion whilst they sought to search into things too high.

Faith is required at thy hands, and a sincere life ; not height of understanding, nor deep inquiry into the mysteries of God.

If thou dost not understand, nor conceive the things that are beneath thee, how shalt thou be able to comprehend those which are above thee ?

Submit thyself unto God, and humble thy sense to faith, and the light of knowledge shall be given thee in such degree as shall be profitable and neces-sary for thee.

3. Some are grievously tempted about faith and this holy sacrament ; but this is not to be imputed to themselves, but rather to the enemy.

Be not thou anxious herein ; do not dispute with thine own thoughts, nor give any answer to doubts suggested by the devil ; but trust the words of God, trust his saints and prophets, and the wicked enemy will flee from thee.

It oftentimes is very profitable to the servant of God to endure such things.

For the devil tempteth not unbelievers and sinners, whom he has already secure possession of, but faithful and religious persons he in various ways tempteth and vexeth.

4. Go forward, therefore, with simple and undoubting faith, and with the reverence of a supplicant approach thou this holy sacrament ; and whatsoever thou art not able to understand, commit without care to Almighty God.

God deceiveth thee not. He is deceived that trusteth too much to himself.

God walketh with the simple,[1] revealeth himself to the humble, giveth understanding to the little ones, openeth the sense to pure minds, and hideth grace from the curious and proud.

Human reason is feeble, and may be deceived, but true faith cannot be deceived.

5. All reason and natural search ought to follow faith, not to go before it, nor to break in upon it.

For faith and love do here specially take the lead, and work in hidden ways, in this most holy, most supremely excellent sacrament.

God, who is eternal and incomprehensible, and of infinite power, doeth things great and unsearchable in heaven and in earth, and there is no tracing out of his marvellous works.

If the works of God were such as that they might be easily comprehended by human reason, they could not be justly called marvellous or unspeakable.

[1] Ps. xix. [7], cxix. [130] ; Matt. xi. [29].

THE END.

PRINTED IN GREAT BRITAIN AT
THE PRESS OF THE PUBLISHERS.